W9-CBN-557

WARP-SPEED
GROWTH

WARP-SPEED
GROWTH

Managing the Fast-Track Business without Sacrificing Time, People, and Money

Peter Meyer

AMACOM
American Management Association

New York • Atlanta • Boston • Chicago • Kansas City • San Francisco • Washington, D.C.
Brussels • Mexico City • Tokyo • Toronto

Special discounts on bulk quantities of AMACOM books are available to corporations, professional associations, and other organizations. For details, contact Special Sales Department, AMACOM, a division of American Management Association, 1601 Broadway, New York, NY 10019.
Tel.: 212-903-8316 Fax: 212-903-8083

This publication is designed to provide accurate and authoritative information in regard to the subject matter covered. It is sold with the understanding that the publisher is not engaged in rendering legal, accounting, or other professional service. If legal advice or other expert assistance is required, the services of a competent professional person should be sought.

Library of Congress Cataloging-in-Publication Data

Meyer, Peter, 1954–
     Warp-speed growth: managing the fast-track business without sacrificing time, people, and money / Peter Meyer.
       p.   cm.
   Includes index.
   ISBN 0-8144-0526-6
   1. Organizational effectiveness.   2. Industrial management.
   3. Corporations—Growth.   I. Title.
HD58.9.M49   2000
658—dc21   99-087908

Printing number

10 9 8 7 6 5 4 3 2 1

Contents

Acknowledgments

Like any growing business, this book would never have happened if any number of people had not been there doing the right things at the right time. John Thompson encouraged it. Dick Heinzelman and Jim Long put their faith in me when no one knew whether there was a business to grow and learn from. They deserve special thanks. Bill Hicks saw this as a book, not a commodity, and changed the way the book works and looks to make it a better tool. It is a better book because of him.

Literally dozens of people put their faith in our consulting firm, helping their businesses to grow faster and more sanely than they might have expected. I mention some of those people by name in this book; others are not identified, for reasons that will be obvious. I would like to thank each one publicly, but . . .

A number of executives, some direct competitors with each other, have graciously worked with us to provide examples. For the ones who were willing to put that aside, I offer special thanks. It is not always easy to decide that you wish to open your business up, and I appreciate the fact that dozens of executives have done that here.

A number of executives and consultants reviewed the manuscript prior to publication. If they had followed my advice, they probably would not have taken the time to do this, so I would like to thank them for their folly.

Several magazines have been gracious enough to let me reprint popular articles that they have run. I owe special thanks to Jan Collins of *Business & Economic Review* and Dennis Organ of *Business Horizons.*

If you don't like the work, none of these people deserves the blame. I do. If you find errors, please tell me so that I can fix them for the next readers. Drop me a line at Peter@Meyer Grp.com.

If you find this work valuable, you should know that much of that value came from the two people who guided the book through countless iterations and rewrites: Ilse Meyer and David Ludwig. Without them, none of the good that is in this book would be in your hands.

Most important of all, there is one person who made this all possible: Eva Meyer. There is no better ground than the earth she walks on.

Thank you. Grow wisely.

Introduction

Warp Speed: "Faster than the speed of light; a science fiction concept explaining how spaceships can travel over vast interstellar distances."
—*Computer Currents High-Tech Dictionary*

Sometimes your business seems to be running faster than the speed of light. As the owner or manager, you call from the bridge, asking your engineer for more speed. You hear about your limits, that "she's giving all she's got."

In TV shows, you still find a way to escape certain death inside an hour. In the real life of your business, even a year is not enough. Just like a spaceship that explores the edges of the galaxy, every rapidly growing business takes on risks and pressures. These increase the chances that your business will fail—vaporized into a cloud of stardust and bittersweet memories. Can your business do better? Just as important, can you *enjoy* growth *and* stay sane?

The answer is yes, if. If you manage the right resources and manage them well, your chances of becoming a long-running series increase dramatically. Warp-speed business growth is unique, difficult, fun, and dangerous. Pulling it off is hard. Staying sane while growing at warp speed is hard, yet immensely rewarding when you succeed. This book is about how to reach and sustain warp speed.

WHO NEEDS A BOOK ON GROWING RAPIDLY BUT SANELY?

Not all businesses will grow rapidly, and as you'll see, there are good reasons your business should restrain growth. But when businesses grow at warp speed, some rules change. Even the verbs reflect this acceleration—all the terms are kinetic. Time gets compressed, costs spiral, people stretch, money and other resources come in fast and go out faster, and some management practices that perform well in gradual-growth companies fail when the pace gets extreme.

This book discusses some key models and tools that will work in such an environment. Not every tool is covered, but the essential ones are here. These chapters provide ideas that may seem odd or counterintuitive but have been proved to work in a rapid-growth environment.

Not everyone expects or wants to grow rapidly, but for two groups of people, the discussion is important. If one of these describes you, I designed this book for you.

✧ The first group consists of managers or owners of an independent company that wants to grow rapidly. This group includes managers who plan on running and owning a fast-growing independent company.

✧ The second group consists of managers or general managers of a high-growth organization inside a larger company. This also includes managers who have their sights set on being the captain of a warp-speed vessel owned by a corporation.

Not all internal divisions are product divisions. You could now be, or plan to be, a branch manager, a service business manager, a vice president with costs and revenues. Your role might be the manager of a country operation for a company that is halfway across the globe. You could be a general manager located in the same building as the rest of the business. If you have, or plan to have, responsibility for costs and revenue for a division and you wish to grow that division rapidly, this book will help you.

In the past, independent companies and internal start-ups faced different challenges. Today the tasks of managing sane and sustainable growth for each are becoming similar. The line between a division and a separate company is getting less distinct. Corporations ask branch managers to run the branches as independent businesses. Independent business owners find that partnerships, investments, and supplier relationships tie them more tightly to larger corporations.

Many organizations and managers switch between the structures and do well. Palm Computing (the designer of the highly successful Palm handheld personal digital assistants) did not do well as an independent company. Short on time, people, and money, the owners sold the business to U.S. Robotics, which sold itself to 3Com for the same reasons. Today Palm is the fastest-growing participant in a rapidly growing market. Palm's founders have left to start an independent company. Switching back and forth used to be impossible. Now it is acceptable.

Is There a Too Fast?

I will not tell you that a certain percentage of growth year over year is correct or sustainable. Rapid is relative. Some companies triple in size comfortably. Some have trouble sustaining 10 percent per year. The object is not to grow at a specific rate. The object is to be able get a rate of growth that is sustainable. Growth that spurts and stops without warning is dangerous for the enterprise. Inconsistent and out-of-control growth must be avoided. This book is not about losing your spaceship but about how to keep it going at a high rate of speed. Warp speed is rapid growth, as fast you can go without spinning out of control.

The definition of *sustainable* will change as your business gets better at managing the resources that it uses to grow. Without an investment plan for time, money, and people, your business may be out of control at 10 percent growth each year. With a plan and good conservation of resources, you might be able to double every twelve months almost indefinitely. The better you are at managing resources, the faster you can safely and sanely pilot your ship.

None of this suggests that you should slow your growth to control it. You may choose to take a deep breath as your spacecraft accelerates, but you don't need to cut the motor. Instead, plan to feed it more fuel. Don't plan on slowing growth; use this book to plan on getting control of the rate of growth you want.

Making It Sustainable and Sane— nvesting from a Foundation

I will build on a platform for sustainable growth. The platform has a foundation, a model called jigsaw management. Working up from that foundation, I'll suggest a structure to manage investments in a growing business. One key principle that has kept successful businesses growing and managers/owners sane is managing the business by managing your investments.

At the speed of rapid growth, every important decision is not just operational; each also represents an investment of resources. That investment takes resources away from other opportunities. Just as with a bank account, if you decide to invest in six-month certificates of deposit, you lose the opportunity to invest those resources in equities. Sane and sustainable growth is a constant balance of investments. The currencies are time and people as well as money.

Not all places to invest these are equally valuable for rapid, sustainable growth. Your strategies matter. Chapter 1 offers an overview of the investment strategies. In Chapters 2, 3, and 4, I'll look at *where* to invest. The three areas that offer the highest return for most growing businesses, and get the most attention in *Warp-Speed Growth*, are:

1. New markets
2. New technology
3. People

What an owner or a general manager invests are resources. I'll build on the platform in Chapters 4 and 5 by discussing time, people, and money, and how to get more of each. There will never be as much of these resources as you want. I'll discuss priorities from the beginning right through to selling all or part of a rapid-growth business.

What to invest leads to where to invest, and then to how to invest. The what is time, people, and money. The where is new markets, people, and technology. The how is applications. (See the list that follows for an example of how the flow works.)

How to invest these scarce resources makes up Chapters 6

through 11. Each pair of chapters first discusses a general strategy and then shows applications of the strategy. The pairs focus on the same three high-leverage areas—new markets, people, and technology—as they build on the platform.

Investment Strategy Flows from What You Invest to How You Invest It

WHAT	*WHERE*	*HOW*
Time	New Markets	
People ➡	People ➡	Applications
Money	Technology	

You'll find specific steps and templates, but you won't find a universal solution for growth. It doesn't exist. This book is designed to show you applications and why they work. You can adapt them to the business you now manage or plan to run.

FOUR BASIC CONCEPTS

Four concepts discussed throughout this book may seem unusual or counterintuitive. Let me briefly introduce each one here and refer you to the appropriate chapter for more details.

Using Jigsaw Management

When you assemble a jigsaw puzzle, do you look at the box top for reference? The answer is almost always yes. But has someone ever given you an assignment that came to you as a bunch of puzzle pieces without a box top? When you aren't growing, this may not be a problem. When you are trying to grow rapidly and sanely, puzzles without box tops can be deadly.

Think of a jigsaw puzzle as the metaphor for planning your resource investments. If you make yourself a picture of where you want your business to go, it will resemble the box top of a jigsaw puzzle, a puzzle made up of hundreds or thousands of pieces. The three tasks of the owner or general manager are to make sure that:

1. The pieces get assembled.
2. The gaps in the picture get filled.
3. No one on your team wastes time on pieces that do not belong.

The concept of using jigsaw puzzles offers an intuitive tool to accomplish these three tasks and grow your business sanely.

Chapters 2 and 4 show you how to use your resources from a strategic viewpoint. Using real cases and examples, you'll see how you can keep yourself and your team sane as you grow. The chapters discuss investment decisions and how to use them to buy yourself more time, people, and money.

Creating and Dominating New Markets

Why the emphasis on new markets? Because creating and dominating a new market is probably the best path to sustainable growth. Creating and dominating a new market is harder than fitting into an existing market. Safety comes from following the lead of others. However, so does a pattern of high competition, tight margins, and slow growth. In Chapters 3, 6, and 7, we will spend considerable time looking at strategies to open new markets.

A market in which you are the only supplier is a market that allows you to increase margins and performance and grow without competition. For growth, high margins and little competition are ideal. However, new markets are hard, and they are a higher-stakes game. You should enter that game with all the skills you can accumulate. This book will help you even the odds when you go to create and dominate new markets.

Investing Limited Resources

Of all the steps that you can take to keep your spaceship intact, managing and conserving resources is the most important. Like the captain of the spaceship, you have a lot of resources, but in times of rapid growth, you don't have enough time, people, or money. You'll want and need thousands of other tools and processes, from a copy machine that works to a faster way to close the books. All of those come from time, people, and money. In Chapter 4, I'll look at why that is true, how to balance the three, and then strategies to get the most from the limited resources that you have. Throughout the book, I ask you to conserve all three. When you or members of your team spend resources in the wrong area, it hurts. Jigsaw management is one tool to help you avoid that pain for your business.

Sleeping Well

Where and *what* you invest come before *how* you invest, and Chapter 3 starts that discussion by looking at a survey of what keeps CEOs up at night. We asked a group of CEOs, and the answers were not what most people would expect. Asking yourself the same question can help you decide where to invest. Making sure the business is always doing the right things, and doing them right, is an ongoing conversation with yourself.

How to Use This Book to Speed Wisely and Sanely

I designed this book to help a practicing or soon-to-be general manager or owner to sustain sane but rapid growth. To use it, start with the first five chapters. These lay out the basic platform on strategy and investments for rapid growth. Where you invest your time, people, and money is where you apply the resources. Chapters 6 through 11 discuss examples of how to apply your limited resources to these areas. The first five chapters focus on the right things to do; the next six blend in a discussion of how to do things right.

Chapters 6 through 11 come in pairs. The pairs are on markets (Chapters 6 and 7), people (Chapters 8 and 9), and technology (Chapters 10 and 11) Each set consists of one chapter on where to invest resources, followed by a chapter emphasizing how. The model the book follows is to discuss the right thing to do and then discuss doing that thing right. It assumes a simple set of steps. Easy to state, harder to do. The book will help you build a plan to do it for your business.

If you are going to grow rapidly, sanely, and sustainably, you should:

1. *Set up a jigsaw box top for yourself and your team.* This tells you in what to invest your resources. More important, it tells you in what *not* to invest. The highest value of the tool comes from telling you and your team what not to do even if it might be attractive.

2. *Identify your resources.* These are what you will invest to make growth happen. You need to have strategies for getting the most from them. Start by deciding which of these resources are the most valuable.

3. *Decide where to invest. Warp-Speed Growth* suggests that there are three areas in which most companies should invest: new markets, people, and technology. Chapters 6, 8, and 10 show you strategies to invest in each. Some of these strategies will seem counterintuitive at first. Nonetheless, they are proven.

4. *Apply the strategies.* I list some applications in Chapters 7, 9, and 11. Even in a book this long, I cannot cover all possible applications, but I hope that I can suggest enough so that you can create your own. Whereas steps 1 through 3 are setting you up to do the right thing, this step consists of doing the thing right without wasting resources. Doing only the right things at minimal resource cost is important and difficult. And when it works, it's fun.

This book is in your hands to show you the details behind the four steps. It focuses on understanding what tools and processes work and why. You will find step-by-step instructions for some applications and tools. They will work, but they are only examples. Business is not paint by the numbers; it is a sometimes spontaneous application of guidelines and tools by an artist. This book will show you, the artist, some interesting tools and guidelines. How *you* apply them is the art—and the fun. Let's start by looking at what goes on when you grow your business rapidly.

WARP-SPEED
GROWTH

CHAPTER ONE

Sustainable and Sane Business Growth

Growth can save you. Growth can drive you crazy: It can spurt and sputter; it can be sustainable; it can kill your business.

Which of these occurs is not up to chance. It is up to you as the owner or manager of a growing company or an "intrapreneurial"[1] division inside a company. You can grow a business in a rapid and sane manner. It does happen, just not often enough. *Warp-Speed Growth* gives you strategies and tools that can help you stay sane while growing rapidly, wisely, and sustainably. If you have profit-and-loss responsibility now, or plan to, this book shows you models, strategies, and applications that can help you sustain growth and maintain sanity.

Many people want their business to grow no matter what—until it happens and the business swells out of control. If you have been there, you know the feeling. Suddenly more is happening than you can keep track of, tasks that should get done don't, and things that should never have happened are happening every day. You rely on key people, but you don't see them often enough. You rely on key results, but you don't have time to make sure you are getting them. You used to buy Altoids;

now you buy Mylanta. You wonder whether your kids still live at home, and they wonder the same thing about you. The business is growing. The questions are:

✧ Is this growth sustainable?
✧ Are you staying sane?

Two Avoidable Problems

Two problems occur when your business grows out of control, and you can avoid both. Problem 1 is that the company is at risk. The common scenario is that you begin to miss details, and that causes you to lose time. Perhaps you have to redo a product. Or a sale falls through. Maybe you have to spend more time and money on customer service than you planned. Maybe you don't have the time to get the best people around you, and it costs you some time every day to make up for that.

Individually, no one of these problems requires much time. Yet as a whole, the cost in time adds up quickly. And as with a footrace, a small amount of time is the difference between winning and losing. The details that you miss start to cost much more than you can afford. Perhaps that small amount of time makes you second in market acceptance. A small amount of time could be enough to wipe out a profit. Maybe you don't have quite enough capability to make something important happen. An important product does not do well because you missed a detail. You grew too fast, and now you can't keep up. Your business suffers and is at risk.

Problem 2 is that the owners and managers are not having fun anymore. Your spouse used to complain that your company ran you, not vice versa. When you grow out of control, even that isn't true anymore: Your growth is running you. It isn't sustainable; it feels (and is) insane. Each owner or manager gets to make a choice about whether to be sane or insane in his or her business.

Many business owners and managers complain that their fast-growth business is not fun anymore. This book is not about enjoyment, but never forget the value of fun. When you recruit employees or contractors, don't you look for people who will have fun doing the work? Don't you feel better when your best people are enjoying their work? Don't they produce better results? If the answer is yes, the same applies to you.

WHY GROW?

For most managers, the question "Why do you want to grow your business?" elicits the response "Because I have to!" People expect growth, with valid reasons. There are also some very valid reasons *not* to do it. (See Figure 1-1.)

The worst reasons to grow are:

✧ Everyone else is.
✧ It feels good.

Few experienced managers choose to enter a market because it seems popular with other vendors or to use a product design because it feels good.

Figure 1-1. Avoidable problems of growing fast.

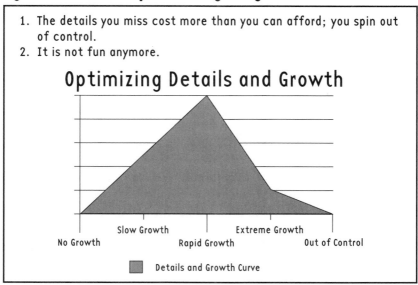

1. The details you miss cost more than you can afford; you spin out of control.
2. It is not fun anymore.

Optimizing Details and Growth

Slow Growth | Extreme Growth
No Growth | Rapid Growth | Out of Control

▨ Details and Growth Curve

These two reasons are poor. However, whether you run an independent company or a branch or division of a larger company, you may choose rapid growth for good reasons. Gaining investments is an example. When you show ongoing growth, attracting both dollars and support is much easier. Your funders and sponsors will expect and value growth.

The same applies to the equity markets and leveraged buy-outs. If you want to attract investments and get the highest valuation for your business, rapid but sustainable growth will be important. If you had to borrow money to open your doors, then the growth may be necessary to cover the burden of debt.

Growth can generate cash flow. Sometimes, not always, that generates more profits. As we will discuss, rapid growth can cost more than slower growth. When that happens, profits may diminish when you grow.

Another reason to grow might have to do with a corporate sponsor. Companies are always looking at a larger goal when they fund an internal start-up. That larger goal may be to:

* Gain market share
* Protect another business
* Raise cash quickly

If you are running a division of a larger corporation, your decisions on products, staffing, and profitability could be subject to the need to grow. You may need rapid growth to keep the support you want.

People are drawn to growth. It helps in recruiting. Growth is associated with winning, and all employees want to join a winner. Rapid growth makes it easier to attract good employees and, at the same time, makes them necessary.

Finally, growth is a marketing tool. In the same way that employees enjoy signing on with a rapidly growing company, so do customers. Many customers prefer to buy from a growing vendor. In a tight sales competition, your growth pattern may be the deciding factor. That may not make sense, but not all purchases occur because they make sense.

Four Fallacies of Growth

As good as growth is, it does not solve all your problems. Here are four fallacies about growth.

Four Fallacies of Growth

1. You can grow out of an operational problem.
2. Growth equals profitability.
3. Profitability improves when every customer is yours.
4. If you grow, the customers will benefit.

Fallacy 1: You Can Grow Out of an Operational Problem

Although you might hope to outgrow operational problems, it doesn't work that way. Operations are not like product costs. Volume may improve your product costs, but if you can't fix the operational problem today, it will get only worse as you increase the volume. Poor yields in today's production will decay even further as you add more people and products. If your information services infrastructure is barely adequate today, it will crater as volumes increase. If closing the books on time is hard now, it will get harder when you grow.

You cannot grow your way out of these issues. If you are growing rapidly, it is critical that you correct these problems early. You do not want to be like the toy company that had to close its warehouse during the Christmas season because the volume was greater than the computerized inventory system could handle.[2]

Fallacy 2: Growth Equals Profitability

If growth did equal profitability, Starwood Hotels and Resorts would be the richest company in the country.[3] Growth does not create profitability. To grow, you will make trade-offs that may reduce your profits to get revenue. Worse, if your growth comes from acquiring new customers, those customers may cost you more to get than the ones you already have, which leads to the third fallacy.

Fallacy 3: Profitability Improves When Every Customer Is Yours

Getting extra customers usually costs you more than it did to get the original customers. There was a reason they did not buy from you earlier. Overcoming that reason costs time, money, and people. Don Potter[4] of Windermere Associates studied this in depth. He looked at 240 lines of business, identifying the top four competitors in each. He then looked for a correlation between being the leader in market share and the leader in profitability.

With four competitors, each market share leader had a 25 percent chance of being the most profitable. A strong correlation between share and profitability would be a number much higher than 25 percent. After compiling the numbers, Potter found that only 29 percent of the market leaders were also the profitability leaders. He points out that Steelcase leads the market in office furniture, but HON leads in profit. Wal-Mart may have the dominant share in its niche, but Family Dollar and Dollar General are more profitable. Market leaders have to stretch to get the extra customers. That reach results in customers who cost more to get and keep. Growth in customers can result in lower profits.

Fallacy 4: If You Grow, the Customers Will Benefit

One common mistake growing companies make is to become very self-focused. It feels as though customers were flooding in. The success is so intoxicating that the company starts to boast about growth to customers, treating it like a benefit that customers will enjoy. A quick glance through business advertising will show you ads that boast of growth as a benefit to new customers.

The opposite is true. Growth per se is never a benefit to the customer. It may enable new locations and products that can be good for customers, but your business could probably gain those customers at a lower cost without growth. Every second of time that you invest in your own growth for its own sake is time that your business could have invested in customers, and they know it. Resources that your business could have applied to make their experience better seem to them to be invested in self-promotion. Smart customers know that growth can be disruptive. They will want to know what you are doing to minimize that disruption.

The worst case is that you are insulting your customers by focusing on yourself. Consider the scenario of the new parents who show you pictures of the family. One picture is fine; several are still OK. However, when you try to change the subject and they insist that you look at more pictures, it gets old. If the parents insist even more, it gets insulting. Yet we rationalize the same behavior with our own companies as though it were a benefit to the customer.

Growth can be great, but only if you tailor your strategies around the reason for growth, not just the growth itself.

What Constrains Sane Growth?

Your business will always have constraints on growth. Resources—specifically, time, people, and money—define these constraints. You need enough of each resource to get growth to happen, and your business never has enough. When you treat all three as investments, you start the process of growing sanely.

In any business venture, you have only three resources to invest. How well you invest those resources will be the deciding factor for how sane and sustainable your growth is. Each of the thousands of decisions you make as you grow is a commitment to invest people, money, or time. They are the currencies of your opportunity.

One of the most desirable ways to achieve sustainable growth is to create and then dominate new markets. This is a holy grail for CEOs of start-ups and multinational companies and a main focus of this book. Recently my firm surveyed CEOs of rapid-growth organizations and asked what kept the top executives up at night. Almost universally, creating and dominating markets is one of the two top issues on the CEOs' agenda.[5] Other issues that get a lot of attention in management and leadership journals do not seem critical in the day-to-day life of a rapidly growing business.

It is easy to see why creating and dominating new markets is attractive. Maintaining a profit in existing markets is difficult. The barriers that might keep others out of your market never seem high enough. Competitive activity constantly drives marketing costs up and operating margins down. A way out of the crunch is to create and dominate a new market, one in which you have no competitive pressures. Once you do, like Microsoft with Word for Windows and Glaxo Wellcome with AZT,[6] you can maintain healthy margins. As the creator of a new market, you can gain some control over your growth.

Growing with Jigsaw Puzzles

One of the most difficult issues for a growing company is applying resources to goals. Identifying and quantifying the resources of time, people, and money is only part of it. Making decisions on how to use them on goals is the next part.

This is not limited to your own decisions. To have sane and sustainable growth, you want your people (employees, contractors, partners, and vendors) to make decisions for you. You can't make all the decisions, and somehow you have to ensure that they are making good ones.

It is a bit like a jigsaw puzzle. If you have all winter, you can do a puzzle yourself. When you have a limited amount of time, you use the help of others. When you do that, you want to keep them involved with the least effort on your part. Most puzzlers do two things to accomplish that: They show the picture on the box top to their help, and they let the help choose how they will assemble the pieces.

One common denominator of a successful fast-growth business is that the executives who run that business are good at ensuring that the box top is clear and visible and stays that way. Then they make sure that they hold their people to that box top without telling them how to hold to it.

This model, jigsaw management, is not the only such construct that can help. However, I will focus on this one, if for no other reason than that it is simple. If you can understand a jigsaw puzzle, you can keep this model in your head and explain it to others. Any model that you cannot keep in your head is too complex for a fast-growth situation.

If jigsaw management helps you to create a foundation (see Chart 1–1), then your investments in time, people, and money are the vehicles to fund growth. You can invest those resources in a variety of areas; we will focus on new markets, technology, and people. Of course, it is too easy simply to say, "Invest time in new markets." If investment strategies are to be useful, you need both the strategies and then examples of applications of

Chart 1-1. Platform chart for sustainable warp-speed growth.

Chapter 12	*Warp-Speed Growth: Managing a Business Built for Speed*							
Chapters 7, 9, 11	APPLICATIONS ☞	Pricing	Tailoring	Prospective rewards	Indies	Prospective appraisals	Killer apps	Pain
Chapters 6, 8, 10	INVESTMENT STRATEGY ☞	Strategy—new markets		Strategy—recruiting and structure			Strategy—effect before technology (change is bad)	
Chapters 1–5	WHAT TO INVEST ☞	Time		People			Money	
	WHERE TO INVEST ☞	Create, dominate new markets		Technology			People	
	FOUNDATION ☞	*Jigsaw management—Building a box top Deciding and communicating what to work on and what to let go*						

those strategies. Building up from the foundation, you have a set of tools to build into growth. Let's start there.

NOTES

1. *Intrapreneurial* refers to an organization that is set up to act in an entrepreneurial manner, but as a division inside the corporation. Sometimes such divisions are referred to as skunk works or incubated companies. The original IBM PC came from such a division, set up to act entrepreneurially inside the larger company.
2. This is a true story about a major manufacturer of plush toys, but the company would prefer not to be identified.
3. Starwood had the greatest increase in revenue among the *Fortune* 500 companies from 1997 to 1998. However, the most profitable company for the same period was Ford Motor Company. Starwood made $1.255 billion in profits for the period; Ford made almost eighteen times as much—$22 billion. Data from *Fortune* magazine online (www.pathfinder.com/fortune/fortune500/index.html).
4. From a study by Don Potter of Windermere Associates, Inc. The study was summarized in "Is Bigger Really Better?" published in *Bridge News*, June 17, 1998.
5. Survey done by The Meyer Group, with results published in "What Keeps CEOs Up at Night?" Peter Meyer, *Business & Economic Review* 44, no. 1 (1997): 9–11. Please see Chapter 3 for a more detailed discussion of that survey.
6. AZT (zidovudine) is a drug commonly used for the treatment of HIV.

PART ONE

The Foundations

CHAPTER TWO

Jigsaw Management: Conserve Time, People, and Money

When your business grows rapidly, you never have enough time, people, or money. Getting more always requires trade-offs, paying out one resource to get more of another. Rapid and sustainable growth forces two critical questions for the business:

1. How can you conserve each resource?
2. How can you get more resources at a reasonable cost?

With so many imponderables, many managers and owners of growing businesses delay this discussion until they need the resources. The unknown future makes advance planning incredibly difficult, and deciding which resource is going to be more important seems impossible. But if you focus on some key decisions now, you can get a much better deal when you go to look for resources from others. This chapter introduces a model to help executives and staff decide which resources to conserve over time. Chapter 4 looks at the resources in more detail, discussing how to make the day-to-day trade-offs. Chapter 5 looks at where to go to get more resources and how to buy them.

Questions That Lead to Sustainable, Rapid Growth

- ✧ How can the business best conserve time, people, and money?
- ✧ How can the business get more of each?

JIGSAW MANAGEMENT—BUILDING FROM BOX TOPS

Start with how you manage cash. When managing money, you don't know where the market is going, but you still plan an investment strategy. You may choose to diversify risk, focus on one sector, or balance a portfolio for high income instead of long-term growth. The actual day-to-day investing stays within that strategy. The strategy tells you what *not* to do.

Your business needs an investment strategy for rapid and sustainable growth. The difference is that you are investing more than money; you are investing time and people as well. You need a tool to define where and where *not* to invest. This tool is not just for the general manager or owner. Present it to the large team of people on whom the profit-and-loss manager depends. Those people will invest more resources, so they need to know the business's investment priorities just as clearly if you want to conserve resources.

Just as in investing, without such a strategy, you'll get some successes, some failures. To get *repeatable* success with decisions, you need to be able to establish a framework within which everyone should be working. The framework defines how the business invests resources in markets, people, and technology. (See Chart 2-1.) That is the purpose of the jigsaw management model.[1] Jigsaw management is a crisp way to deal with management and communication decisions. The model is easy to use and can be kept in your head. It helps to reduce waste of time and resources. Best of all, if you are familiar with jigsaw puzzles, you are familiar with the model.

Chart 2-1. Platform chart for sustainable warp-speed growth.

The strategies to use resources well are all based on the box top. The box top becomes the foundation for investing and conserving resources.

Chapter 12	*Warp-Speed Growth: Managing a Business Built for Speed*							
Chapters 7, 9, 11	APPLICA-TIONS ☛	Pricing	Tailoring	Prospective rewards	Indies	Prospective appraisals	Killer apps	Pain
Chapters 6, 8, 10	INVEST-MENT STRATEGY ☛	Strategy—new markets		Strategy—recruiting and structure			Strategy—effect before technology (change is bad)	
Chapters 1–5	WHAT TO INVEST ☛	Time		People			Money	
	WHERE TO INVEST ☛	Create, dominate new markets		Technology			People	
	FOUNDA-TION ☛	*Jigsaw management—Building a box top Deciding and communicating what to work on and what to let go*						

USING THE BOX TOP

When you put together a jigsaw puzzle, what is the first thing you do? Before you start the edges, do you look at the box top? Most people do. It gives a clear picture of what they are trying to re-create. Now consider work assignments that you have gotten over the years. Answer these three questions:

1. Has anyone given you an assignment that did not come with a box top?
2. Would it have been easier with a box top?
3. Would the business have saved time, people, or money if you'd had the box top?

The clearer the picture, the more easily and quickly you can work the puzzle. The box top is what allows a person or team to decide where a particular piece belongs. It helps to determine which pieces do not belong in the puzzle and can be set aside. This reduces waste of time, people, and money.

Every day enormous amounts of data surround us. Look at your in-box or the agenda of your staff meetings. As with puzzle pieces, we must sort and organize all these data if they are to be of any use. A business day resembles an extended jigsaw puzzle. Disconnected pieces of potentially valuable information appear, and the team members must arrange them into a comprehensible picture. The faster your business grows, the faster the data appear, and each piece of trivia, data, and random noise requires a decision—whether to deal with the bit or not. This decision is about where, and where not, to invest resources.

Jigsaw puzzles require similar decisions, such as how to start or what to do next with all those pieces. The task of the owner or general manager is to make the box top clear, to build the foundation shown in Chart 2-1. For three examples, let's look at how an airline solved an investment issue, how a capital equipment manufacturer used a box top to determine its warranty policy, and how the CEO of a growing hospital manages her agenda.

Ask the CEO About Drink Carts?

Jan Carlzon became CEO of SAS[2] as it unexpectedly began to hemorrhage money. Asked to return it to profitability and growth, he faced hundreds of decisions. The challenge: How could he get each of those decisions made without wasting time, people, and money?

Early in the job, Carlzon found himself looking at a $2 million decision to buy new food carts for the planes. This decision had been taking time and attention away from the carrier's executives for more than five years. Proponents argued that new carts would improve customer service and flight attendant morale. Opponents argued that the carrier couldn't afford either the expense or the message it would send to the employees. Carlzon delayed the cart decision to work with his team to develop a box top. (See Table 2-1.)

The box top they chose: to become the premier business traveler's carrier in Europe. It was a decision that quickly helped them to direct their resources. It provided the foundation for an investment strategy.

Making box tops is not an exact science, although you can make it more precise. Carlzon's objective was not to create a metric but to direct his team's investments. By telling his team to build an airline focused on business travelers, he made it easier for them to decide quickly which pieces to work with and which to ignore. Investment decisions got simpler by limiting options. For example, creating a new city stop to attract tourist traffic looked attractive but just did not fit the box top. It would absorb time, people, and money that were not expendable if SAS were to grow.

The management team members eliminated large costs from their business by simply asking whether such costs would help business travelers choose their airline. Management delayed or dropped many investments. However, the decision to spend $2 million on food and drink carts to improve the experience of business travelers was an easy and automatic yes.

Table 2-1. Carlzon's box top and the drink carts.

Box Top	Question	Conclusion	Decision
Become the premier business travel airline.	Spend money on drink carts?	Business travelers care about getting the right drink—and quickly.	Invest in drink carts.

What Is the Right Warranty?

How much warranty to offer is another of those decisions that gets discussed to death in many organizations. Low-cost and consumer products often come with a "complete satisfaction" warranty. Since the sunk cost of a sale is low, complete satisfaction is a relatively inexpensive offer and can differentiate a company. It was important in helping Amazon.com and Nordstrom grow. But a warranty is more difficult with capital equipment. A strong warranty is expensive. Customization and installation costs are lost if customers return the equipment. Some equipment suppliers offer no warranty at all.

For years the management team of BigTel Industries[3] argued over what kind of warranty a company that sells industrial machine products worth millions should offer. (See Table 2-2.) The CEO asked Michael Hepworth, president of Hepworth and Company, to measure satisfaction among BigTel's customers. Hepworth suggested that BigTel might want to measure *dis*satisfaction, exploring why customers didn't buy from BigTel.

Table 2-2. BigTel's box top and the warranty.

Box Top	Question	Conclusion	Decision
Become the supplier of choice.	Add an expensive warranty?	New customers would be attracted by a strong warranty.	Offer a strong warranty.

To decide how to judge success, Hepworth asked BigTel's definition of satisfied customers. Since no one had a definition, Hepworth asked BigTel's CEO to set the box top to focus his team. The response: "To build relationships with clients, to ensure that we are the supplier of choice." This simple statement defined success for the first time inside BigTel. It allowed Hepworth to establish a meaningful measurement system and ignore hundreds of side issues. It also provided the necessary foundation for the warranty decision.

Hepworth's team measured customer dissatisfaction levels and the cost to become "the supplier of choice." Hepworth's customer research showed that warranty clearly fit in that definition, and BigTel chose to offer a strong one. For this company, a stronger warranty will build more sustainable growth.

Keeping the Executive Agenda on Track

Creating a box top does not guarantee that it gets followed. One reflection of how much attention the box top gets is the calendar of the owner or general manager. As an experiment, I asked several owners and general managers of growing businesses to give me an overview of their box top and a glimpse at their calendars. One came from a hospital, which is not a typical growing business in the late 1990s and early twenty-first century.

The strategic plan for the hospital is shown in Figure 2-1. When you ask CEO Teri Fontenot to describe the Woman's Health Foundation box top, she will tell you that Woman's is a place where you go to be treated individually as a woman and enjoy the experience, as seen in Table 2-3 on page 22. "The mission of Woman's Health Foundation is to create opportunities that improve the health status of women and infants." The concentration is on practicing reproductive medicine and on reaching the community. Fontenot's operational focus is on ways to promote special experiences.

The hospital has attached specific plans and numbers inside this framework. For instance, the financial strength objective is to raise $15 million in capital by a set date.

Note the substantial limitations of scope. The programs are focused on women's and children's issues. Woman's provides inpatient treatment for breast cancer, for instance, but not for lung cancer. Obstetrics is a focus area; orthopedics is not. The box top that management draws for the doctors, staff, and community is one that clearly eliminates activities.

Fontenot uses that as an advantage. She balances her schedule carefully, with an ongoing focus on the issues in that box top. For instance, like most senior managers, she wants to be available to her staff. She channels that via Woman's focus on birth. Each month she has breakfast with the staff members who have birthdays in that month. And she does not miss these.

If you look at Fontenot's daily schedule (an example of which appears in Figure 2-2), you will see that it runs full. The

Figure 2-1. Strategic plan for a growing hospital.

WOMAN'S HEALTH FOUNDATION STRATEGIC PLAN

I. **CORE GOAL I**
BUILD PREMIER WOMEN'S AND CHILDREN'S PROGRAM IN REGION

A. Provide high-quality and innovative OB/GYN programs and services to capture regional market share.
B. Selectively expand service offerings to increase market presence.
C. Increase outreach services to expand regional presence.
D. Strengthen key relationships with other providers and payors.
E. Invest in infrastructure to support building premier program.
F. Selectively increase national recognition through Research Institute.
G. Strengthen relationships with employees.

II. **CORE GOAL II**
CREATE TIGHT INTEGRATION WITH MEDICAL STAFF TO MAINTAIN COMMITMENT

A. Continue to upgrade facilities, technology, and operations to attract physicians to Woman's campus.
B. Continue to involve all physicians in governance and management.
C. Evaluate building of Physician Tower II to accommodate additional physicians on campus.
D. Explore expansion of practice support services offered to physicians.

III. **CORE GOAL III**
ENHANCE FINANCIAL STRENGTH

A. Significantly increase capital reserves over the next decade.

IV. **CORE GOAL IV**
WORK WITH COMMUNITY TO CONTINUOUSLY IMPROVE THE HEALTH STATUS OF WOMEN AND CHILDREN

A. Take a leadership role in getting involved in and supporting women's and infants' health initiatives.
B. Partner with other organizations to expand community-based initiatives related to women's and infants' health.

Figure 2-2. One day from Teri Fontenot's agenda.

Thursday, June 24[1] 7:30 A.M. to 8:30 A.M.	Breakfast with employees with birth-days in June
8:30 A.M. to 9:30 A.M.	Review renovation plans for surgery and patient rooms
9:30 A.M. to 10:00 A.M.	Dr. K., B., N., J., to discuss physician gainsharing (your office)
10:15 A.M. to 10:30 A.M.	J., A., J., fetal monitoring strip access in physicians' offices
10:30 A.M. to 11:30 A.M.	Review agenda, materials, and finan-cial statements for hospital board meeting
11:30 A.M. to Noon	Medical staff survey results
Noon to 12:30 P.M.	Visit labor and delivery unit
12:30 P.M. to 2:00 P.M.	MD lunch at Chalet Brandt—7 doctors from medical staff [part of a commit-ment to meet informally. Lunches are scheduled periodically—any doctor who wishes to do so may come.]
2:15 P.M. to 3:00 P.M.	Regent's Advisory Council conference call (American College of Healthcare Executives)
3:00 P.M. to 4:00 P.M.	CEO of Baton Rouge Area Foundation to discuss board nominees for Founders and Friends [the fund-raising cam-paign]
4:00 P.M. to 5:30 P.M.	Chamber of Commerce Executive Com-mittee meeting [Fontenot is the trea-surer.]
5:30 P.M. to 6:30 P.M.	Meeting to discuss scope, function, and resources to be allocated to re-search (Chair of Board, Chief of Staff, VP Medical Affairs, MD Director of Re-search Institute)
7:00 P.M. to 9:00 P.M.	Symphony annual meeting [Fontenot is the outgoing treasurer.]

strategic plan links most of the items that made it onto her calendar. It is interesting to look for meetings that were proposed but did not make it onto the schedule. Many day-to-day operational issues are not here: she has traded the community involvement for the operational focus. This requires a different set of people resources, and Woman's has invested heavily in excellent medical administrators. Now Fontenot invests her time in the community, creating experiences, and the capital fund.

No executive lives in a perfect world. Some activities stay on Fontenot's schedule that do not directly relate to the box top. She has an hour to prepare for the board meeting. It has to be done. Many owners or general managers wouldn't decide to invest an hour on renovating rooms. She focuses on creating experiences, which kept that particular hour on the agenda.

Table 2-3. Fontenot's box top and the calendar.

Box Top	Question	Conclusion	Decision
A place where you go to be treated individually as a woman and enjoy the experience.	Spend time on room renovation?	Room renovations will substantially affect the patient's experience.	Leave it in the agenda.

Saving Resources

Carlzon, Hepworth, and Fontenot each used a similar concept to make decisions easier for the entire enterprise and to eliminate waste of resources. An SAS executive wanted to increase profits by modifying planes to carry more cargo. However, the box top of an airline catering to business travelers suggested a low priority for the time and people investment required to support that idea. If one of BigTel's managers suggested cutting the availability of spare parts to reduce costs, executives would measure the idea against the box top of becoming the supplier of choice.

When your company is not growing rapidly, your team has plenty of time to evaluate these ideas and do cost-benefit analysis. In a rapidly growing business, it hurts to invest in something outside the box top. A person-week here or there *is* a big deal when growth stretches your business. Ideas, no matter how attractive, that do not fit, should be dropped. You don't have enough time, people, or money to chase each alternative.

SAS, BigTel, and Woman's gained other advantages by using this kind of model. The model also affects the culture of the company. At SAS, Carlzon cleared a decision that had taken undue time and energy for five years. Are there issues in your business that take up meetings and pull analysts off more important projects? How often do people review the equivalent of the cost and benefit of drink carts? Getting to a decision quickly doesn't just save the resources for that decision. If done often enough, it has the potential to change the tone of your business so that it emphasizes speed and responsiveness.

If your team is assembling a puzzle with a time limit and real penalties for being late, the team will have little patience for any extra pieces. Time limits and penalties happen in your business, too, and you should have little patience for wasted resources.

Whether you use jigsaw management or another model is not as important as getting there. Use a tool to display where your business should focus time, people, and money. Make sure the people investing your resources understand where to make their investments.

Box Top, Mission, and Vision

Box tops are similar to mission statements and vision statements, but like the cover of a jigsaw puzzle, they are much more limiting. Missions and visions can be (and often are) intentionally nonspecific. Many growing companies have missions that are similar to the one that Steve Jobs discussed at Apple in the early days—to create a computer for the people. Some are as general as "to be the best vendor in the X market."

The box top of a growing business should be considerably more specific. In the early 1960s, many people may have suggested that we needed to explore the planets. The President issued a more specific challenge: to walk on the moon by the end of the decade. It was more than a vision; it limited and focused the effort in the same way you would target an aggressive business initiative.

Jeff Hawkins and Donna Dubinsky of Palm Computing had a mission to build a successful palmtop computing product. It was Hawkins's specific design limitations that made it actionable. He set four goals that he would not negotiate. The Palm-Pilot had to[4]:

1. Be tiny and thoughtlessly portable.
2. Be able to communicate seamlessly with a personal computer—an accessory, not a separate computer.
3. Be fast and simple—the primary competition would be organizers, not PCs.
4. Be able to sell for less than $300.

Without a clear definition of mission, contrasting mission with box top is difficult. Nonetheless, we can clearly delineate some characteristics that a good box top should have.

What Makes a Good Box Top for Growth?

Businesses create good box tops and poor ones. You will want to test yours. Start by identifying the most important objective for your business. For Carlzon, it was to become Europe's leading carrier for businesspeople. For others, it might be to:

- ✧ Create and dominate the [name of new market].
- ✧ Become the grocery chain of choice to [name of specific market].
- ✧ Develop real estate projects that return all the financial investment within X months.

Each of those box tops would eliminate a variety of other decisions and possible investments. For example, if you select a specific market for your grocery chain, it allows you to ignore other markets. The market need not be geographic; it can be defined by customers. Do you want the customers who buy at warehouses? Who buy only organic? Who prefer brand names? Who prefer service? The choice of one of these can eliminate several others. A good box top narrows focus.

We have been rather imprecise about box tops so far. By getting more precise, we can improve the box top. Of the many ways to get more exact, start by attaching success criteria to the goals. Adding a success criterion changes Woman's goal of significantly increasing capital reserves to a box-top border of raising $15 million in a specific period. Striving to reach $20 million would reduce the resources available for other goals. Hepworth can quantify BigTel's goal of becoming the vendor of choice as capturing X customers who do not yet buy from the company by the end of the next fiscal year. More than X would be good but not worth more to BigTel than other uses of the same resources.

Many owners and general managers set success criteria by asking, "How will we know when we are done?" and setting a number to the answer. The question takes considerable thought to set a measurable answer. However, if you don't, you run the risk of wasting time, people, and money in "creeping elegance." For example, BigTel set itself the goal of reducing the waiting time for customers calling the help center. The staff spent several months creating options and scenarios that would reduce the waiting time to varying levels without coming up with a plan. When the senior executive for the operation set specific success criteria, the list of options dwindled. Many options would not deliver that number; many would overachieve. Only two or three would hit the target. The decision got much easier for the team. The investment in setting a limit helps conserve resources you will need to grow rapidly and sanely.

Some managers never set achievable numbers, encouraging the team to exceed expectations. Although this can work well in sales, it can be very expensive elsewhere. If 100 percent is all you need, investing time, people, and money to get to 110 percent will increase your opportunity cost. BigTel can get the call waits to zero, but if it is growing quickly, the resources might be much better used creating and dominating a new market. Using success criteria tells your team when to stop investing resources in unnecessary elegance.

SMART and Important

As you consider what you want your business to do, look for the following characteristics in a box top:

✧ *The box top is Specific.* As with a picture on a puzzle box, all the people you work with have to be able to see it. A vague box top will deliver vague results, wasting resources that the business could use to sustain rapid growth. The owner or general manager owns the responsibility for preempting ambiguity.

✧ *The box top is Measurable.* You will know when you are achieving it. "Significantly increase capital reserves over the next decade" is not as effective as "Raise $15 million by January 1."

✧ *The box top feels Attainable.* Don't build something so grand that no one will work for it. Jeff Hawkins of Palm Development used to walk around with a wooden block in his shirt pocket, asking people to build a PalmPilot that big but no larger.[5] If he had talked about building a wired world, team members would not have known where to start or how to limit decisions. His company would have built hundreds of prototypes that were never used and wasted time, people, and money.

✧ *The box top clearly tells people where* not *to invest Resources.* Hawkins's decisions clearly limited the scope of development. He was careful to tell people what not to invest time in, such as a PC card port or a printer driver.

✧ *The box top includes a clear Time element.* It tells people when they will be done and ready for the next box top. By implication, if not explicitly, it tells them how much time they have to get there.

✧ *The box top is Important.* Don't invest in any efforts that are not. If sigma 6 quality is not truly important, why spend dozens or hundreds of person-years to get there?

The box-top model carries a danger. What if the business has no overriding vision or box top? If it does not, how does a manager in your company make key decisions? How does he or she know how to save resources and avoid time-wasting projects?

The answer is that your company can't share in those benefits. Sane and sustainable growth will get that much harder. Some executives do not have a box top defined, and for them, poor or slow decisions are indicators of this. Managers must develop and present a clear picture to their employees and associates. It will always be individual, but that is what Carlzon, Hepworth, and Fontenot did.

The faster your organization grows, the more dependent you are on how well you and those near you can make decisions. If you can eliminate decisions that do not need to get made and speed up the ones that do, you will add sanity to your days and your business's growth. Setting the box top creates the foundation for your investment decisions by telling you *where* to assign your resources.

NOTES

1. Peter Meyer, "Jigsaw Management," *Canadian Business Review* 22, no. 4 (1996): 17–19. As discussed in the article and used here in adapted form with permission from The Conference Board of Canada.
2. The SAS story is taken from Carlzon's book *Moments of Truth* (New York: Harper and Row, 1987).
3. The company is real, but the name has been changed.
4. Taken from a profile of Hawkins and Palm Computing in the article, "In the Pilot's Seat," in the *San Jose Mercury News*, November 10, 1997.
5. For more on Hawkins, Palm Computing/3Com, and box tops, please see Chapter 10.

CHAPTER THREE

What Keeps the CEO Up at Night: Worries of Not Finding New Markets and Good People

Where and *what* you invest come before *how* you invest. This chapter looks at where and what by asking, "What keeps the CEOs of growing companies awake at night?" If you are (or plan to be) an owner or a general manager of a growing company, this is a question you want to ask often. You want your team to ask it often as well. When you find that the answer does not match the box top of the business, consider this a signal to adjust the focus of the business or the team—to make sure that you are doing the right thing as well as doing things right. The answers appear twice in the path from box top to application (Chart 3-1). They are where you can plan to invest your business's resources. Once you choose that, they can become strategies as well.

Where are some likely focus areas? New markets offer less competition, a better chance to define a vision and make that

Chart 3-1. Platform chart for sustainable warp-speed growth.

New markets and people are two key areas to focus investment.

Chapter 12	*Warp Speed Growth: Managing a Business Built for Speed*						
Chapters 7, 9, 11	APPLICA-TIONS ☞	Pricing	Tailoring	Prospective rewards	Indies	Prospective appraisals	Killer apps / Pain
Chapters 6, 8, 10	INVEST-MENT STRATEGY ☞	Strategy—new markets		Strategy—recruiting and structure			Strategy—effect before technology (change is bad)
Chapters 1–5	WHAT TO INVEST ☞	Time		People			Money
	WHERE TO INVEST ☞	Create, dominate new markets	Technology				People
	FOUNDA-TION ☞	*Jigsaw management—Building a box top Deciding and communicating what to work on and what to let go*					

vision a standard. People are what make results happen. Even if this seems obvious, it makes sense to look at empirical data as well. Before I chose these two, we called a group of CEOs and asked them what keeps them up at night.[1] The results are here in this chapter.

I'd suggest two good reasons to look at what these CEOs focus on. The first is that it gives you a chance to compare the academic answers to the empirical. Many concerns that the journals identify as critical to growth aren't critical to the practicing executive.

The second is that you can gain quick lessons from watching CEOs worry. Just because something keeps another executive up at night does not mean that the same concern should leave you counting sheep. However, knowing what is at the top of the executive agenda does give you three opportunities to help grow your business more sanely. Curing executive insomnia can help you:

1. Target your business more quickly and successfully.
2. Get more value from your team.
3. Obtain better results at lower prices from your suppliers.

The first opportunity is to target your own business more clearly. Like you, each of your customers or clients has more than one problem to deal with during the day. Like you, they rank these problems. They try to work on the most important one first, then the second most important, and so on. If you know how to solve the tenth problem on your customer executive's list, you are valuable. If you know what the top two or three problems are and can help solve one of those, you can be both valuable and expensive. That value can translate into higher volumes and higher margins. Knowing what is likely to be at the top of their lists will help you stay focused on fast-growth opportunities. Working only on your customer's top two or three problems helps your business to grow quickly and sustainably.

The second opportunity from focusing on what gives executives insomnia comes from your team. Whether they are direct employees or part of your larger network, you will benefit if your team focuses on the top problems as the customer sees them. Sane growth is easier when you get your team to focus on the top problems as *you* see them. With only so much time in the day, if they spend it on less important issues, both your company and your customers lose.

The third opportunity comes from your suppliers. They invest considerable resources in trying to gauge what you will buy. If they are busy presenting products that attack the tenth problem on your list, show them the top problems and ask them to work on those instead. It will help you grow if you can show them what to develop and present to you.

These three opportunities are useful for practicing general managers and owners as well as for managers who plan on taking responsibility for profit and loss. The strategies and the thinking behind them will also be useful for those who would advise and support general managers and owners. You will find a few paragraphs on those strategies at the end of the chapter. But first, what issues appear at the top of the CEOs' list of priorities?

SLEEPLESS IN THE EXECUTIVE SUITE

To get the answer, we interviewed executives who run growing manufacturing and service companies across a variety of industries on several continents. We asked them to tell us the two problems that keep them up at night. It is a simple question but one that most of the CEOs had not been asked. More than half of them found the question interesting enough to respond immediately. All wanted to know what the others said.[2]

You might hope for a pattern from which to learn, and sure enough, such a pattern exists: two problems come up in almost every conversation with CEOs of growing companies:

1. Creating and dominating new markets
2. Getting and keeping the right people

Of the two, new markets are the bigger concern.

Creating and Dominating New Markets

The axiom is that the first company to define a market has the best chance of dominating it. These executives are focused on doing exactly that. They put great emphasis on trying to define a future market through the company's own vision and technologies. This might seem the purview of the marketing departments, but the company presidents feel the need to focus on it personally.

The president of one systems company hopes to use dominance in one market to define the standards in another market. "The idea," he said, "is to get the wireless providers to follow the standards adopted by the wire-line companies." These happen to be standards that were partially set by this supplier. If it can get the new companies to define their needs in line with these norms, this supplier "can use one architecture to grow the business." By defining the standards for a new market, this company can be the first and dominant supplier in that market. This is very much to the company's advantage. In this president's view, it is too important to delegate.

Many executives talk of trying to set the rules of competition for a new market, because setting those rules can make it easier to establish dominance. The president of a network products company said his priority was defining the ground rules for a new set of technologies. "Can we capture the high ground and mind share of the buying community?" The head of a growing service provider wants to set the standards for the "governance and use of Web control [and] the smart use of technology to do that."

Each individual market has different ground rules. What one set of customers absolutely needs, another will not value. That creates unique problems when you wish to develop new markets. Your management team has to decide which rules can and cannot be ignored in a market that no one yet knows. And it has to be done quickly, before you invest too many resources in the wrong rules.

Reliability is a good example. Getting extreme reliability is not critical for most customers. If a supplier of Internet browsers ships an early version that is only 90 percent reliable, users adapt and accept. However, telephone companies and data communications customers will not allow that. Their products have to be so reliable that users can measure downtime in minutes or seconds per year.

This unique need has a defining effect on how some of these CEOs try to develop those markets. Mature products are often more reliable, but building a new market cannot wait for mature hardware and software. This complicates the process of creating a new market to dominate it. Several CEOs interviewed were trying to work through the issues of exactly how much reliability to have before they enter the market. One executive worries over the comparative values of "being first to get to [and define a] market against waiting to be highly reliable. How do you balance those?" Walking this tightrope keeps several of these executives up at night. Investing too heavily in the wrong direction could result in the wrong products getting out the door or could make the company late to market. It could cripple the results and stunt growth for years.

The common lore is that senior management is very focused on ways to cut costs. However, none of these executives have bloat on their lists. To these executives, risk is a different issue. Risks, when they appear, focus on markets and growth.

A top Japanese CEO looks at it differently. "We are entering a new world. Absorbing new information is a problem. Do we really know the market?" This executive is focused on "industry and technology trends to help guide headquarters' directions." Instead of trying to imprint the market with his technologies, he wants to "keep our eyes and ears open and not miss important trends." Yet even here, "we have new products, but the market is not ready yet."

His response is to share the risk with partners. As difficult as this is, he is more worried about missing the growth opportunity than about costs. With him, as with almost every other executive, opportunity costs outweigh operating costs.

Finding and Keeping the Right People

The CEO of a quickly growing manufacturer responded, "First has to be keeping great people and then attracting more of them." Most of the other CEOs said something similar in first or second position.

To a president in the U.S. Midwest, recruiting is a team responsibility that cannot just be left to the human resources department. "Things are not what they used to be. Acquiring and retaining people is the most important thing we can do."

Another general manager is "frustrated that we are trying to do more than we can. Things could go better. Some people do not give a s——t. Finding and keeping the right people" is the first objective on that executive's list.

"The thing that limits our ability to grow is finding and keeping people," says the chief operating officer (COO) of one dominant supplier. This is so important to his company that it is moving key software from a proprietary code to one that is more attractive to prospective employees. This is a fundamental and expensive change, one that customers had not asked for and that has little value to the customers. Worse, if something goes wrong, it will threaten the company's ability to deliver new products, which, in turn, could threaten the business's ability to grow quickly. So if a change will cost a lot of money and may threaten the company's ability to meet targets, why would the COO demand it? Two reasons override those concerns. One is to enter a new market, and the other is to improve the company's ability to recruit and retain good people. That latter is the driving force for changing software platforms.

The CEOs do get concerned with recruiting and benefits, but those are not the issues that keep them awake. They all have teams who handle recruiting and benefits for the companies. The value these CEOs feel they have to add is to make the work attractive and interesting.

Changing the software code is not a decision that human resources would make. It is a concern that a business unit head must consider. Getting good people to come and stay is, when all is said and done, as much a quality-of-work issue as it is a benefits issue. The right people come here when the work is more interesting. It is not an HR decision, and the CEOs we interviewed make a point of involving themselves in quality-of-work decisions.

Benefits and income will go only so far, but these executives are concerned with making the work itself more interesting. Employees will leave for more benefits or pay, but they stay for better work.[3] Making work more interesting is a line management responsibility, not something with which human resources or training can help. These executives are looking for and using ways to increase satisfaction on the job. (For some techniques that work with rapidly growing companies, please see Chapters 8 and 9.)

WHAT DID NOT MAKE THE LIST?

Most of the management fads of the 1990s are not issues that keep CEOs awake. Quality was not mentioned once. Customer service did not make the top two or three. Empowerment was not on the radar. Reengineering never came up.

Hot Topics That Did Not Keep CEOs Awake

✦ Vision and leadership
✦ Mergers and acquisitions
✦ Time to market
✦ Cost cutting
✦ Quality
✦ Risk reduction
✦ Customer service
✦ Empowerment
✦ Reengineering
✦ Enterprise resource planning software
✦ Year 2000

The only time these issues came up was when they directly affected creating new markets and getting and keeping the right people.

DO THE SURVEY RESULTS APPLY TO OTHERS?

I surveyed CEOs from publishing, insurance, software, telephone services, and education. Defining and controlling markets and getting and keeping good people were top in the responses in all these fields. For example, Jerry Ascolesi, president of a major insurance brokerage, quickly responded with:

> What keeps me up at night?
> A. How do I continue to provide a long-term secure environment for our employees?
> B. What products do we develop and value-added

services do we come up with [to] develop a better mousetrap to make it unique to our industries? [Doing that] allows us to have an incredibly high retention ratio and to develop a high level of service. We do not want customers to come to us one year and leave the next.[4]

New markets and the right people were the top concerns of every CEO interviewed. You might think it safe to assume that new markets and the right people are likely to be near the top of the lists of your customers and prospective customers as you grow. The odds will support your assumption. However, as with any assumption, you should check this one by asking the question of the CEOs who you hope will become your new customers.

If your business is approaching a new market or a new customer, you would be smart to ask early. It could change the sales cycle for an individual client or the product definitions for a new offering. More fundamentally, you could fine-tune the whole new-market definition so that it works with fewer of your resources. Asking "What keeps you up at night?" could make the difference between quick success and a long struggle in a new market.

THE VALUE OF THE QUESTION

One interesting result from this survey was that many executives find the question just as interesting as the answer. To the CEOs, the question "What keeps you up at night?" has value in itself. Asking it of others shows several traits that differentiate your business from others. When you or your sales team asks that question, it gives your company three advantages:

1. It increases differentiation and may increase your margins and revenues.
2. It reduces the cost (to you) of creating and entering new markets.
3. It increases your ability to create a new market.

First, it implies that you have decided to focus on the customer's business with the same intensity with which you focus on your own. Most suppliers don't show or do this. The whole premise of the customer-focus fad in the early 1990s was that companies don't pay enough attention to the needs of customers. Despite thousands of articles and hundreds of books and speeches, that has not changed across businesses. The company that focuses on customers and customer issues is still rare, different, and valued. Remember that at the end of the day, people buy from people. And all of us will gravitate to people we like. We all like people who are interested in us. When someone sincerely wants to know "What keeps you up at night?" it shows an interest in you.

Second, the answers can help you reduce your time and cost to develop a market or a product that matters. Too many companies hope to grow by developing a solution and then finding out who really has the problem. Developing solutions in search of problems results in products that are hard to sell and need extra time to position. You expend development, sales, and marketing resources that could be better used elsewhere. By asking what keeps the buyer up at night, you learn what you can present that will be of greater use to the market—whether it be one company or a new market. With that information, you can target your business efforts correctly and skip much of the wasted expenditure of resources. That will reduce the cost in time, people, and money of making a sale or creating a market.

The third advantage is that it will show you where you can create new markets. When you find a trend in a group of customers, you may have found a market that is ready to launch. If you can tap that market, you can find the same holy grail for which all the CEOs in this survey are looking. Since the customers want the solution badly, you can deliver it at a larger margin for your business.

WHERE DOES RISK FIT?

One key to survival is judging and handling risk. A key to maintaining a crisp vision of your business is to focus your offerings on the area of highest leverage. Helping a client reduce risk can be very high leverage. The problem with these statements is that most of the CEOs we talked with have a different view of risk.

Most businesses have risk management and audit functions. The CEOs surveyed in this study are just as risk-averse as the rest of us. However, to promote growth, they take risks that the auditors and others would avoid.

For an example, look at the income restatements by software companies in the 1990s. Some came from new interpretations of rules by the Securities and Exchange Commission (SEC), but many restatements came from companies that had clearly taken risks with how they reported revenue. The consequences had disastrous effects on some industry leaders at the time.

Is it possible that the CEOs and CFOs of these companies were ignorant of the risk? Were the audit committees unaware of the risk? Instead, it seems reasonable that the internal staff raised the issues, and after consideration, the CEOs nonetheless decided to report the revenue that way.

Risk goes beyond reporting data. The COO quoted earlier in the chapter risked his revenue flow to switch to an open software platform. In a different conversation, Alan Naumann, president and CEO of Calico Commerce, told me that he had intentionally refocused his company after measuring the risk—losing focus and customers as the company is beginning to really grow—against return.[5] Why did he do it? His top three concerns[6]:

1. "It will add 50 percent to our long-term market valuation."

2. "It helps us in the recruiting of new employees."

3. "If we had not done this, there would have been significant opportunity costs in new markets" (to many software companies, a strong position on Wall Street helps build a strong position in the minds of customers).

Are there risks? Certainly. Will Naumann look at them? Yes, as they relate to the valuation, recruiting, and opportunity costs. Risk to many managers involves incurring dollar costs, losing a project, or losing a customer. Risk to these CEOs involves losing a market opportunity or losing the chance to recruit and retain excellent people.

Use Lack of Sleep to Grow Your Company

Worries that keep you up at night can help you grow your business more sanely, even if your own answers are different from those of the CEOs we interviewed. Whether or not these problems describe what keeps you awake at night, you can use the question ("What keeps the CEO awake at night?") to focus your:

- ✛ Negotiations
- ✛ Management team
- ✛ Sales force
- ✛ Vendors

Negotiate Strategy

You may be negotiating an acquisition, a contract, or a price. If you accept that it is good negotiating practice to focus on the other person's needs, you are only halfway there. When you are negotiating with another CEO, how do you know what those needs are? Too often you *assume* when you should *know*. You gain two advantages when you ask what keeps the other party up at night.

First, you move the negotiations away from minutiae and into broader business issues. This can help you set the correct ground rules for the conversations and keep the right topics on the negotiating table. If you are negotiating to buy or sell a business, you can be discussing growth of the overall business instead of the price of the components.

Second, the question shows you to be a person more likely to consider the perspective of the other party. If you are negotiating with someone who thinks that you will give value to his or her side, it makes it easier for that person to give value to yours.

In your next negotiating session, ask the other side how *its* markets are changing. What does it need to do to define or get to these new markets? Can your company offer something that will help the other one create a new business without a competitor? If so, that support could be worth much more than a few more dollars or shares in one deal. You will be helping to create value where none existed before.

Save Time—Manage Your Own Team Better

As a leader, you gain real value when you let subordinates know what keeps you awake. A good president won't give priority to concerns that are less than critical to the business. What is important enough to be on the top of your agenda should be important to the company. If one of your people knows what keeps you up at night, he or she can help deliver the answers that will help you and your stockholders sleep peacefully.

But are the people who work with you focused on something besides what is truly important? They may be doing many things right, without doing the right thing. The result is fractured effort when your business barely has time to get the right things done if you all pull together.

Direct Sales Teams

Whether your sales team works directly for your business or is a separate channel, asking "What keeps the CEO up at night?" can help achieve sustainable growth. This question can help increase your margins as well. Ask how the sales team starts a sales process. Does your team lead with cost savings and technical superiority? Wouldn't you prefer your salespeople to approach projects in a way that can help your customers grow their own businesses?

If the sales team is talking about technology or how to do something cheaper, customer CEOs may want to delegate the discussion to others. When a sales team leads with a way to grow the business, then the CEO is much less likely to delegate.

Consider showing the sales team how *you* buy. Do you focus personally on purchases that help you get to market acceptance sooner? Do you delegate technical buys? Use your own approach as an example your sales team can appreciate.

Directing the sales team this way can improve your margins. If your sales team is addressing issues less important to your customer CEOs, you may be discounting to get sales. When your people are not solving problems that presidents find compelling, they are not working on the issues of greatest importance. That makes it difficult to use "added value" to justify a price.

Get More from Vendors

A discussion of what keeps the senior manager awake is bound to get the attention of any wise vendor. Such a supplier will want to build its sales and delivery plans around the customer's needs. As the customer, that can work to your advantage.

If your suppliers know what keeps you up at night, they can craft a solution that truly helps your company. If not, they are likely to focus on their own company. That will not be of much use to you.

TELL EVERYONE THAT *YOU* CAN'T SLEEP, AND TELL THEM *WHY*

Whether or not the results of the survey describe what keeps you awake at night, you can use them to focus your team, your sales force, and your vendors. Start by handing this book to them and asking whether new markets and recruiting and keeping the right people top their lists. Then tell them the two top priorities in *your* mind. Ask them to find out the same information from your customers and prospective customers.

Ask your people and vendors to forget common lore. Cost cutting is not the key to the executive suite. All these CEOs have people to keep costs down. However, most get personally involved in dominating markets and in getting and keeping the right people.

You will always find a hundred reasons not to share your concerns with employees and suppliers. You'll find a hundred more reasons to ask your sales teams to focus on your own needs instead of the issues that keep your customers awake. Let me suggest an overriding reason to share your concerns and to direct your sales teams to understand the concerns of others: what is of highest concern is what gets done. Make sure that everyone knows what keeps you up at night.

Rapid growth is difficult. There is no point in making it harder by working on the wrong areas. The key to success will be investing time, people, and money correctly. The places to invest include new markets and the right people, as defined by the box top for your business. You might also invest those resources in technology (discussed in Chapter 10) as well as in areas that I do not cover in the book. But before *where* to invest, a rapidly growing business must look at *what* to invest. In the next chapter, let's add some detail to growth and resources.

NOTES

1. Peter Meyer. "What Keeps CEOs Up at Night?" *Business & Economic Review*, September 1997, pp. 9–11.
2. Participants in the survey were promised that their answers would be treated confidentially.
3. In 1999, InformationWeek Online surveyed 21,398 information technology professionals—one of the white-collar groups that is the most heavily recruited across industries. It found that the strongest incentive to leave or change jobs was the challenge and responsibility of the work. Base pay was the third factor on the list. (© April 26, 1999, by *Information Week*.)
4. Conversation with the author.
5. Conversation with the author.
6. Conversation with the author.

CHAPTER FOUR

Rapid Growth and Your Resources: Knowing What to Invest

Rapid and sustainable business growth is hard. You are working to meet the needs of a present that never really exists and a future on which you can't count. As the demands get greater and greater, sanity seems to evaporate.

Of course, the symptoms have causes, and this chapter deals with some of them. It also discusses the resources you invest to keep growth sustainable and how to choose which ones to value most highly. This chapter is primarily about those resources and using them well.[1] This chapter discusses *what* to invest; the following chapters discuss *where* and *how* to invest.

Growth varies in magnitude. Your business might experience gradual growth, rapid growth, or extreme unsustainable growth, each of which I define in this chapter. No single metric applies to those terms. Doubling in size may be rapid growth for a company like Amazon.com that is in a hot market. It might be extreme for Woman's Health Foundation. Doubling might be a little slow for a company opening a new market. It can change by year: your business will be growing comfortably at 150 percent per year as it ramps up in the first two years, but as you reach the third year, 75 percent growth might be hard to maintain. It will be different for separate parts of a company. Although 3Com may be stressed at 50 percent per year growth, the Palm Computing division of the company was focused on exceeding 100 percent growth. It is not the number that matters; it is your ability to sustain it.

Growth gets out of control, gets that insane feeling, when the demands for time, people, and money outstrip access to them. Demand and supply are important to a growing business from an internal as well as external perspective. Externally, it will always affect your product mix and pricing. Internally, the supply of your key resources constrains you. Any business runs on resources. Some of them come from you and some from others, but the business always faces limits. Your resources have to be budgeted and invested wisely. That is the key to sane and sustainable growth.

What Restricts the Growth of Your Business?

Disgusting as it may be to have to admit this, your business can't do everything. Each business has limits, and so does each entrepreneur or manager. Whether a start-up or a market leader, each company makes choices about what it will and will not try to do. Choices must be made about:

- *Time:* what the leaders hope that they can get done in a given year
- *People:* what the company can hope to do with the abilities and bandwidth[2] the staff has
- *Money:* what each effort or project gets to spend

The choices are critical. A mistake can plunge your business into bankruptcy; the correct decision can make for years of success. The choices never stop because as you grow at warp speed, your business never has enough resources.

For most executives, this may seem intuitive. But consider an example. In 1990, WordPerfect dominated the word-processing market for desktop computers. Growing dramatically, the company had decisions to make about where to allocate resources for development, service, and marketing. In general, the decisions were working. The company and its products continued to be the standard against which others were measured. IBM (with DisplayWrite) and Microsoft (with Word) were trying to gain share but without much success.

Simultaneously, the operating system market was changing. (Operating systems are the underlying layer of software that gives a computer the ability to run programs. They also set the standards for how information is displayed and handled on the screen.) The new Windows operating system used an entirely different way of working with a computer, a standard set of interfaces and commands. It was very attractive to users.

WordPerfect had a choice. The company could divert more people and money into adapting to the new operating system. Or it could continue to invest in new features, sales, support, and perhaps alliances with other vendors. What the company could not divert was time. The development of Windows wouldn't slow because WordPerfect was not working on it. The amount of time the company had to respond was limited.

Microsoft had more time. The developers of Word knew that Windows was coming. What they did with that head start was to invest people and money in a Windows-based word-processing product. The company wanted to have the first widely accepted Windows word processor. Microsoft invested in Windows, while WordPerfect invested in DOS.

As of this writing, Microsoft's share of the word processor market is approximately three times the share of all others combined. IBM dropped DisplayWrite and bought the Lotus version. WordPerfect was sold to Novell and then again to Corel.

No one can know whether WordPerfect would have retained its market dominance if the company had chosen to invest in Windows products earlier. However, you can see the effect of limits. WordPerfect could not do everything. Even as the market leader, it had to make a choice about where to put limited resources. In the end, that choice mattered a great deal.

THE TASK OF THE OWNER OR MANAGER

The task of the person who owns or manages a growing business is simple to state: You not only have to do things right and do the right things, you have to make sure you are *only* doing the right things.

Focus is the mantra of many advisers, but what do you focus on? You can focus on operations, markets, technology, sales, costs, and dozens of other facets of your business. Each of these is important, but the amount of resources your business can allocate to them controls the chance of success. If you start with the amount of resources to supply to the critical projects, the operational focus will be easier and the business can stay in balance. Start wisely by starting with your resources.

It is the task of the owner or general manager to go beyond doing things right. Most people can focus on and are good at that. But fewer are good at doing the right thing. Tracking that falls on the shoulders of the senior executives. The business moves forward through systematically investing critical resources in the right way and in the right places. Everyone does investment management, but someone has to make sure it is always done correctly. That is the owner or general manager.

WHAT HAPPENS WHEN YOU GROW FAST?

Growth is a special state for your business. To most managers, it feels good, and then, as the pace picks up, it feels like hyperspeed. You take orders faster. You have to build product faster. Then you have to ship more orders in the same time. As you do that, you have to find more materials in the same time. Though you can buy cheaper in quantity, cash goes out faster and faster. To compensate, you have to invoice and collect more aggressively, or cash gets even scarcer. Simultaneously, you need more people to catch up to the new level of activities, and finding them consumes time. When you find them, it costs more to get them.

Simultaneously, your infrastructure becomes stressed. Your building is full. There are not enough electrical outlets or pads of paper. Tactical problems are getting in the way all day long. Your computer systems become inadequate. You need time to choose new ones and more time to install them, debug them, and learn how they operate. Then you need time to tailor them.

As the product ships, you need more service people. Because you have more customers, you need to listen to them and communicate with them. To do that, you need more marketing people. Because they have good ideas, you will need more product development people to put the new ideas into a form that you can deliver. If the product needs to be tested, that means more people to test it and to make sure that it really does work with the product you shipped last year. Then you need people who can sell both the old and the new product. They need to be trained and managed. The faster you grow, the faster all this happens.

As you grow, the pressure to grow again continues. Getting more money from others and getting more and better people are both easier when you can show sustainable growth. You know that your lenders and investors of both money and people are more likely to work with you if you double in size each year.

All of this takes money, too, but as you look at what needs to be done, the money seems the least of it. Suddenly, time looms as the hardest resource to manage and conserve. You work long hours, and so do your best people. People take pride in sleeping at the office, in taking more red-eye flights. You expect your people, and yourself, to spend sixty or eighty hours on the business each week. After a while, you wonder what is wrong when you don't.

You know that you are not as productive after twelve hours as you are after six. Intuitively, you sense that decisions made at 2:00 in the morning may not be as well thought out as those made at 2:00 in the afternoon. But if you do not put in the time, what will happen to the business?

THE COSTS OF GROWTH

The good news about not growing is that you don't need to invest heavily in additional resources. Steady state means you can get by with the same or similar people. With little growth, you can predict your costs. You can anticipate where time demands are likely to come from and you can respond accordingly. Your time is under your control. However, when you decide to grow, your ability to anticipate goes down as the need to invest increases.

When you decide to grow, the need to invest increases. Gradual growth requires resources. Rapid growth requires a disproportionately larger share of resources. Extreme or out-of-control growth consumes resources intensely, more quickly than you can replace them. As we examine the three states of growth in the following subsections, consider where you would rather be.

Characteristics of Gradual Growth

The most important characteristic of gradual growth is that you can plan for it. You can predict a need for money or people to meet a project or customer requirement. This allows you to forecast your needs well in advance. You can get resources in time and at a reasonable cost. (See Figure 4-1.)

For example, if you have new products coming, you can forecast the need for new salespeople and predict the point at which you should have them in place. Will you need salespeople about six months before the new product is ready to deliver?

Figure 4-1. Demands on resources.

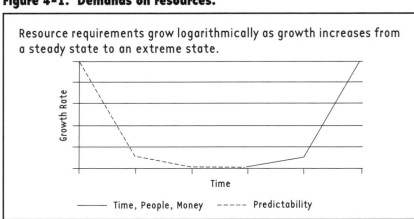

You can look for them in advance and do it at a reasonable cost. If necessary, you can choose to wait a little for the right people to come along at the right price.

Gradual growth is like building a skyscraper from a complete set of drawings. The business develops a plan and runs according to the plan. You spend your time on plans to fill this building with profitable tenants and to construct the next skyscraper.

Characteristics of Rapid Growth

Rapid growth is harder to plan for. As with a fast-track building, you are working without complete drawings. As you build the third floor, the architect is still designing the upper floors. You'll get done faster, but you'll spend considerably more money and energy to get the result. You'll make some mistakes and invest resources in some poor places because you didn't know what the architect would wind up doing. Those mistakes are the cost of rapid growth. The result is good, though: each floor sits on top of the underlying one, and you get use of the building sooner. You make a trade, investing more of your time and money to get quicker returns. Of course, you need to make sure you maintain enough quality to support the return.

In the new-product example, you know the need for salespeople is coming, but you don't really have the time to get the sales team lined up in advance. You compromise. Perhaps you use outside reps, or you hire people who have either more or less experience than you need. Maybe you use more expensive resources from inside your business. If you or the vice president of sales is up late at night writing the boilerplate of a proposal, does this really save you money? You have expensive resources doing the work that would cost your business less if you could just do a little more planning. You don't get twice the work done for that higher cost. You just get the same amount of work done on time.

Often, this is the perfect trade-off. You invest more time and money to get into a market sooner than if you were more deliberate. You will pay more in time and money to be there, but it is an investment that can give you excellent returns.

You can adapt well if you use the strategies that I discuss later, but you are always paying a premium for rapid growth.

Rapid growth is a juggling act. If you are not careful, you'll drop balls. One of those balls represents new opportunity. The biggest danger of rapid growth is that you will miss an opportunity because you are moving too fast to get to it. The definition of rapid growth will vary from business to business, but let me suggest that when you get here, "rapid" is as fast as you want to go. This is warp speed, very fast but under control. No matter what the internal or external pressures, avoid extreme growth.

Characteristics of Extreme Unsustainable Growth

Sometimes growth spins out of your control. Instead of you running your business, it runs you. You are doing things that you never planned, and they cost a lot of time, people, and money that you didn't allocate and probably cannot afford.

If you are erecting that multistory office building, you can't build on top of the newly constructed stories because you didn't design the lower floors with the right reinforcement. Instead of going up, you find yourself adding wings and extensions that you never planned. They don't really match, and yeah, the overall effect looks ugly, but you got it done.

If you are launching a product, you find yourself adding and deleting features right up to the last minute. The marketing team is trying to get sales to call on the best long-term customers first. Under pressure to perform quickly, the sales team is calling on whoever they think might generate a sale this week or quarter. Salespeople make promises to make sales happen. The development and support teams are wondering how they are going to deliver even half of what marketing and sales are promising. Even when they figure it out, they may never get the product quite right, but they will work lots of hours to backtrack and re-create as they attempt to keep up. Doing and redoing are the common element, and everyone takes it for granted. Now you have your key players working harder but doing the wrong things. It costs more time, people, and money, but that is the price of extreme growth. Yeah, it looks ugly, but you get it done.

If only that were all. Because the salespeople are trying to get every warm body excited, they are going to be calling on people who will be wrong for your offering when it is ready.

Worse, if they do not use the correct priorities to decide whom to call, sales teams will escalate requirements for features and changes to please customers that you would rather not have. No one is working to create the opportunities you really want.

The sense of compromise and spending resources spread. When the vice president of sales calls the support manager to ask for just a single meeting with that marginal customer, who is going to say no? Again, you have your key players working harder but doing the wrong things.

The gamble is that this work will position you better for the future. Burning off resources now will be worth it because it will enable you to be there tomorrow—wherever "there" is. The cost is high. You not only miss opportunities, you miss details that you need in order to take maximum advantage of your business's current opportunities.

In extreme growth, you may trade customer satisfaction for time. When Netscape was an independent company, it released early versions of its browser regardless of whether they were fully tested. The growth rate demanded that people work around the clock, even sleep underneath their desks. The company released the product on time, but in a beta stage—not fully integrated or tested. It became the consumers' responsibility to wait or test the browser for Netscape. Not all users were happy to perform product testing.

The same phenomenon seems to have occurred with large turbine engines. In an attempt to deliver more turbines faster, the suppliers may have cut back on testing, letting users perform the tests in return for early delivery.[3] From the customers' point of view, the manufacturers may have sacrificed quality for time. The results can vary from uncomfortable to untenable.

Part of extreme growth involves a state of contradiction. Events are happening so fast that you reach the point at which you can't even invest in yourself and your business anymore. No matter how many people you add and how much money you throw in, you do not have time to put those resources to work.

Extreme growth eats up resources faster than you want to know. It is not just money; it is people and time. People and time can help create and then respond to other opportunities. What happens to a business when it cannot create and respond to opportunities? When that happens, the company will be passed by a company that can respond. A company that misses opportunities may find that it cannot survive.

GROWING WISELY—YOUR THREE CRITICAL RESOURCES

The good news (and the bad news) is that you have only three resources to invest in a rapidly expanding business: time, people, and money. These are the currencies that buy you opportunity.

With rapid growth, you don't have infinite money, people, or time to do what you want in your business this year. You have the choice of either allocating those resources or letting them go to the first person who asks.

Compounding this, extreme growth creates a state that might be termed "resource allocation by noise." Just as the noisiest wheel gets greased, the noisiest requester often gets the resource. As the volume of requests increases, you lose your ability to hear what is right. Your ability to manage your business wisely and sanely quickly follows.

Sane and sustainable growth requires you to allocate not only your money wisely but your people and time as well. This allocation is the most important role a general executive has. How do you decide how to allocate?

INVESTING YOUR RESOURCES WISELY

The best use of resources is not to spend them as requests come in but to plan to invest them as you use them. It is the same with cash: you are always balancing where to allocate money against the return to the business. The best use for cash is a topic that gets a great deal of attention. People and time deserve the same attention, or more.

While developing a pharmaceutical drug, a marketing manager might want to increase initial sales by offering the compound as a pill, an injectable form, and a capsule. You only have so many people capable of designing delivery systems. The decision to offer one or all three is an investment decision in which people are the currency.

Time can also be spent or invested. If you recently attended a meeting that did not seem to do much good for you or your work, you can identify with the cost of a wasted hour. Time is, first and foremost, a business resource. To create and dominate a market, you will want to choose a point in time to enter the market. At that moment, you'll want to have hundreds of tactics and events complete. The time required to make them happen will be a critical resource. You will need to respond to market changes and competitive threats. It will be a real advantage to be able to do so as fast as you want. If you hear that a competitor is considering entering, you will need time to think. What barriers do you want to erect (such as drop a price, tie up the largest customers, or request regulatory changes)? Perhaps you should abandon the market yourself. Then you will need time to take action, even if that action is as simple as raising a price on a Web site. Time is a controlling factor to strategy; without enough time, the best strategy cannot succeed.

Your business can trade these three resources (time, people, and money) back and forth. With more good people, you gain some time for your own work. With more people who need your attention, you lose that time again. You can invest money in people instead of infrastructure. You might offer a better benefits package or use a more expensive contractor to do your marketing work. You can use your own time on projects to reduce the need for more people.

The opportunities for trade-offs are nearly infinite. Some make sense; most don't. The fastest way to avoid wasting time, people, and money is to rank the resources according to the value they deliver to you. Then you can invest them in the areas and strategies that give you the most return.

WHICH RESOURCE IS THE MOST VALUABLE?

Time, people, and money are not equally valuable to a growing business. You can and should set priorities for conserving them. At times, you might trade people to get more time, or money to

Chart 4-1. Platform chart for sustainable warp-speed growth.

A key to investing well is to understand the relative values of what you are investing.

↑	Chapter 12	*Warp-Speed Growth: Managing a Business Built for Speed*							
	Chapters 7, 9, 11	APPLICA-TIONS ☛	Pricing	Tailoring	Prospective rewards	Indies	Prospective appraisals	Killer apps	Pain
	Chapters 6, 8, 10	INVEST-MENT STRATEGY ☛	Strategy—new markets		Strategy—recruiting and structure			Strategy—effect before technology (change is bad)	
	Chapters 1–5	WHAT TO INVEST ☛	Time	People				Money	
		WHERE TO INVEST ☛	Create, dominate new markets	Technology				People	
		FOUNDA-TION ☛	*Jigsaw management—Building a box top Deciding and communicating what to work on and what to let go*						

get more good people. Faced with the thousands of decisions that come with growing a business, it gets easier to make the correct decision when you have set priorities among the resources. The opportunities for trade-offs are nearly infinite. The fastest way to avoid wasting time is to set your resource priorities in advance. Time is the most critical of the three resources. People are second. Money is third. This becomes part of your box top and guides your investment decisions. Think of each of these resources as scarce. Consider how difficult it is to get more of any of the three or to recover from a mistake with any of them.

Over the years, I have asked hundreds of senior and middle management teams to rank the three resources, and I get the same two responses almost every time. A typical example comes from Aspect Telecommunications, a midsize high-tech call center software and hardware provider in California.

In a workshop, I asked six Aspect general managers to rank these resources. They chose the same order that most managers do:

1. People
2. Time
3. Money

At dinner that night, Dennis Haar (then the executive vice president) joined the general managers. Before I could pose the question, one of the GMs asked Dennis how he would prioritize the three resources. Dennis quickly answered:

1. Time
2. People
3. Money

The answer was different, and he felt comfortable defending that difference.

Time/people/money and people/time/money repeat as the two answers in almost every instance that we ask about resource priorities in workshops. Most managers choose people first. Most presidents and senior executives choose time as more important than people. Almost everyone chooses money last. (See Table 4-1.)

People, as a resource, carry the highest priority in a lot of academically based literature. Many companies, like Aspect, pride themselves on making people a key part of their culture. With that in mind, Dennis's team challenged his rankings. He listened and, without knowing how other senior executives had answered, stood by his original statements. Time over people is an answer for which field experience contradicts the academic models.

Table 4-1. The most valuable resource—common answers and rankings.

Ranking	Managers	Senior Executives, Presidents
First	People	Time
Second	Time	People
Third	Money	Money

As time went on, Aspect's growth slowed, and the market changed. Dennis became president and then left. As the company continued to try to grow at the same pace, management was careful to identify growth and resource issues. For instance, Aspect's chairman wrote:

> Our Company's Business Focus Is Changing. . . . If we are unable to successfully make this transition in a timely manner, there could be material adverse effect on our business, operating results, or financial condition. . . .
>
> The Prices of Our Common Stock and Convertible Subordinated Debentures are Volatile. . . . Should the price of our securities decline rapidly, we may become subject to class action securities litigation. Such litigation would be a costly diversion for our management team.[4]

These are risk statements that go beyond boilerplate. They resonate with many CEOs of growing companies. Delays and diversions are terribly expensive.

WHY TIME OVER PEOPLE AND MONEY?

Why do many CEOs consider time more valuable than people or money? Consider how difficult it is to get more of any of the three or to recover from a mistake with any of them. (See Table 4-2 on page 58.)

Getting More Money

Getting money is never easy, but hundreds of ways exist to recover from a sudden need. You can steal from some other budget. You can ask for more cash. You can delay another project. You can sell something. You can go to venture or angel markets. You can borrow the money from institutions or friends. You can slow payments to vendors. Both large and small organizations can recover from a cash problem in a few months. Recovering from a person problem is harder.

Getting More People

A mistake in hiring takes much longer to correct. If you hired the wrong person (or the job outgrew him or her), you won't know for months. Once you find out, you have to either help the wrong person grow into the job or move him or her out of it. Either course of action takes more months or even years in some organizations. If you move someone out, you still have to find the right replacement, consuming more months. If the person or role is key, it hampers the growth of your business.

Any mistake in people, no matter who is at fault, will cost you dearly as you try to grow rapidly. You can recover, but the price is measured in months or years.

Getting More Time

But what if you lose time? Even in periods of rapid growth, a person has only sixty to a hundred hours in a workweek. When those hours are gone, you can't replace them. You can't buy back the hours or add them to another week or year. That time has vanished forever. There is no recovery. Time is the most perishable commodity.

Bandwidth always has a limit. No matter how hard you push, the wire and the executive can only carry so much in a given time. With people as with telephone lines, there will always be limits to bandwidth. Time is the most limited and perishable resource. Your task in managing growth is to find ways to use this resource in the best possible way.

Table 4-2. How hard is it to recover?

Error In	Difficulty of Recovering
Money	Hard
People	Long and hard
Time	Impossible

INVESTING TIME—WHAT IF THERE WERE AN EXTRA 10 PERCENT? THREE EXECS RESPOND

You can approach the question of how to invest time from another direction. Ask yourself what your business would do if you could find a way to add as little as 10 percent more time. Consider:

✧ What if you could safely wait a little longer before you froze a product prior to launch? You might use the time to get more customer input or to incorporate a technology that is just maturing to increase function while cutting cost.

✧ What if you could skip half your meetings for the next two weeks without missing anything?

✧ Would 10 percent more time in the field for the members of your sales team allow more bookings in a quarter?

I asked the question of a series of senior executives from rapidly growing companies. The following subsections present answers from Bob Finocchio of Informix, Alan Naumann of Calico Commerce, and Ken Sullivan of Cabletron.

Strategy and Time: Robert Finocchio, President and CEO, Informix Corporation

Finocchio[5] took over as CEO when Informix was at a low point in revenue, profitability, and market value. The company had been growing immensely but was about to restate the financial results of previous years. The result was a large restructuring charge and a restatement of almost a quarter billion dollars.

These amounts were equivalent to the company's entire annual revenue only a few years earlier.

The issues around such a write-off absorbed immense amounts of management time for the first quarters that Finocchio was in charge. They sucked time away from other concerns and led to reduced attention across the company as people focused on whether their projects (or jobs) would survive the next quarters.

If he had had the opportunity to gain more time, Finocchio remarked:

> One, I would focus on strategy issues. You can't just let strategy be passive. . . . I've been forced to accept the top layer, the veneer of strategy. [It takes time to think through questions such as] Are we a software company? A systems company? A tools company? Do we supply computers with software? Should we have a consulting business? How broad?
>
> We missed a few windows of opportunity because of the distractions. For instance, we believe that we had incredible technology for industrial-strength Web sites. But if you asked anyone on the street to name the top ten or twenty—we were not on that list. We didn't have the time to take advantage of that during the period of chaos.
>
> In the [Windows] NT space, we had great products but no market traction. We got the best products for NT out the door, but by then the competitors [were] already there.

More time to plan the strategy greatly increases the chances of getting the products out the door on time.

When Finocchio came in, "We were suffering from schedule morass, time drift." Managing time takes time. It is axiomatic that it takes money to make money, but the statement applies just as well to the resource of time. With that bandwidth, he would find more ways to "use people for leverage. The key [comes when] I can get more from the other 3,499 people" at Informix. Given that extra time, "I would have forced myself and my team to *take* more bandwidth for this. It is a way to get more bandwidth *back*."

For Informix and Finocchio, "time is [the] currency" for keeping growth under control. Using it is key to Finocchio's objective to "end up with a company worth having, a company that people want to work at, that customers will bet their business on."

An Extra Day Each Month: Alan Naumann, Calico Commerce

"When I first thought about this," Naumann said, "I asked if 10 percent was really enough to do something meaningful."[6] Then he worked it out:

> If our managers are working sixty hours a week, that's six hours a week of found time, an extra twenty-five to thirty hours a month. If each executive staff member could use just a third of that extra time to spend a full eight-hour day on [strategy, getting closer to customers, and communication], that could have real impact!

Three areas in which to invest that time:

> 1. Spend more time on developing strategies that won't have an impact for twelve to twenty-four months. [For instance, at the time we talked, the company was establishing a new presence in the market.] Had we not spent time asking fundamental questions, we would not have quickly and consciously changed our market focus and strategy. The changes we made will add 50 percent to our market valuation. It helps us in the recruiting of new employees. If we had not done this, there would have been significant opportunity costs.
>
> 2. Getting close to customers. We have eight executives who each sponsor one key customer relationship within Calico, as in: "What is the best software company that Dell ever worked with?" [And what do

we need to know to be even better?] We do that well now; we are not spending enough time on it.

3. Having each member of [the] executive staff spend some of that time communicating with people in their group "in informal broadband mode."

Alan believes that group meetings are an important way to get information distributed. Although e-mail is good for some announcements, group meetings excel in allowing interaction and in getting "alignment" around key issues and strategies. But they take time to plan and time to hold. "We are hiring so fast, moving so quickly, that we have to overcommunicate, and that takes time.

"There are so many fire drills, crises, and so on to manage. You've got fifteen e-mails when you get in, people waiting at your door. It is urgent, but none of that is about" strategy, customer contact, or broadband communication. "Having an extra eight hours per person per month would be very valuable."

More Response at the Same Cost: Ken Sullivan, Executive Vice President, Global Services, Cabletron Corporation

Cabletron sells and supports the hardware and software that help computers talk to each other. The market in which it operates is known for companies running at the edge of control. One place where you would not want to lose control would be in how you support your customers. Sullivan had been growing[7] the support business more quickly than the rest of the company. When he considered how he would use 10 percent more time for his people, he did not hesitate. "It would go to my 'break-fix' people." He would invest that time in training and helping them deal directly with more customers.

"I don't measure up to world-class standards yet in terms of responsiveness. If I had 30 percent more bandwidth, it would be eaten up doing the same things we are doing today. We'd use it to become more responsive at the same fixed dollar cost."

Sullivan notes that reducing the time your people have reduces your ability to deal with the pressure of growth. This means that you miss opportunities.

THE CURRENCIES OF OPPORTUNITY

When you invest your time, people, and money poorly, it costs you opportunity. This could be such possibilities as:

- ✧ A chance to roll out new products and services
- ✧ The option of adjusting your cost structure
- ✧ An opening to improve your market dominance

The most expensive opportunity cost is the cost of not being able to define and then dominate a new market. New markets are hard to create, and once created, they are hard to dominate. It would be terrible to get started in a new market and then not have enough capability to dominate it. To do it right, you will need as much of the three resources as you can conserve.

The currencies of opportunities are people and especially time. You cannot buy a new market or customer with cash. Good people are necessary to find the opportunities, and the people need time to take advantage of them.

Growth requires fuel. No business or organization can grow without enough of the three essential resources. Too little money, and the right things cannot get done. Too few of the right people, and the money and time become unimportant. Too little time, and all the money and people are useless.

Many problems will not respond to more staff and funding. As Frederick Brooks Jr. points out, "The bearing of a child takes nine months, no matter how many women are assigned."[8] Time is the most restrictive of all the resources. When you are growing wisely, you are conserving time as much as possible and investing it as wisely as you know how. You are making your growth sustainable.

NOTES

1. Parts of this chapter first appeared as "Growing Your Business—Sanely," by Peter Meyer, in *Business & Economic Review*, October 1999, pp. 27–30.
2. Managers in high-technology companies often refer to band-

width as the amount that can be transmitted over phone lines or that a person or an organization can process in a given time. It is always limited.

3. Charles Fleming "Turbine Makers Are Caught in Innovation Trap," *Wall Street Journal*, February 13, 1998.
4. Aspect Telecommunications Corporation Annual Financial Report to Shareholders, March 23, 1999, p. F7.
5. Interview with the author, March 11, 1998.
6. Interview with the author, May 6, 1998.
7. Interview with the author, February 19, 1998. Sullivan has since left to become an executive at Technology Solutions Company.
8. Frederick P. Brooks Jr., *The Mythical Man-Month: Essays on Software Engineering*, anniversary edition (Reading, Mass.: Addison Wesley Longman, 1995), p. 22.

CHAPTER FIVE

Buying Future Growth: Corporate or Private Investors . . . or Not?

One of the most complicated decisions you will make in growing a business is how to get others to invest more resources in your enterprise. Your business may need more time, people, or money than you can gain internally. If so, you may want to look at how to take investors. The decision is not straightforward. You might:

✧ Sell the business.
✧ Spin it off.
✧ Take small or large investors.
✧ Go public.

How to take investors is a question to think through *before* you get forced into a decision. A model such as jigsaw management will be useful in deciding whether and how to sell your business.

Acquiring resources by selling part or all of the business requires your management team to answer two questions: (1) What do you want to do? (2) With whom do you want to do it? Let's start with the first question, using a real example.

Anne's business, The Digital Pen, designs sites for the World Wide Web.[1] Her company is growing quickly, and she wants it to grow even more quickly before that market shakes out. In return for the resources she needs in order to grow the company, she is willing to relinquish some control.

Chart 5-1. Platform chart for sustainable warp-speed growth.

		Pricing	Tailoring	Prospective rewards	Indies	Prospective appraisals	Killer apps	Pain
Chapter 12	*Warp-Speed Growth: Managing a Business Built for Speed*							
Chapters 7, 9, 11	APPLICATIONS ☞							
Chapters 6, 8, 10	INVESTMENT STRATEGY ☞	Strategy—new markets		Strategy—recruiting and structure			Strategy—effect before technology (change is bad)	
Chapters 1–5	WHAT TO INVEST ☞	Time		People			Money	
	WHERE TO INVEST ☞	Create, dominate new markets		Technology			People	
	FOUNDATION ☞	*Jigsaw management—Building a box top Deciding and communicating what to work on and what to let go*						

Growth creates an ongoing conflict between keeping events under control and letting them go. The most successful managers stay involved with what is most important, but the line between involvement and control is very blurry. It gets more so under stress, and most of us are less likely to give up control under stress. When you decide to take investors, the tendency is to focus on the decision to give up some money or equity. Most managers find that the loss of control over their destiny and daily activities is even more difficult. Don't take it too lightly.

If you find yourself looking for an investment in order to grow, don't automatically go to the investment community with hat in hand. Consider a few of the steps that Anne is looking at to strike a better deal. These steps define the box top for her decision.

Three Steps to Striking a Better Deal

1. Remember who is buying here.
2. Choose your currency.
3. Decide *what* you want to buy.

STEP 1. REMEMBER WHO IS BUYING HERE

Start by remembering who is doing the buying. You may call it a merger, a partnership, an investment, an acquisition, or an offering. It means you are giving something up. You could be providing a seat on your board. It might be trading equity away or the loss of some control over your product schedules. The business might pass on an opportunity in order to keep the investor happy. You might pursue an opportunity that does not make sense to you. You are giving something up. The question is: *What are you getting in return?*

Approach this just as you would any major purchase. If you were buying a quarter million dollars of production equipment, you would choose one model over another for very specific reasons. Although some characteristics matter a great deal to you, price is rarely the top criterion in your purchase. Instead, you assign more weight to functional factors that are unique to you and your business.

You are the buyer of the resources that you need to grow. Look at your investor as you would look at any supplier of capital equipment—with one important exception: this investment will cost you more than any equipment you will ever buy. If you want to abandon production equipment, all it costs is money. If you want to remove a partner or an investor, it will be much more difficult.

STEP 2. CHOOSE YOUR CURRENCY

Next you have to decide what you will spend to get the resource. What will you trade to that supplier? In return for some resource, you will give up control or a market or rights to a product or a technology. If you conduct an initial public offering (IPO) for cash, you remain the CEO, but now you have a boss—the stock market. You have to answer to analysts, Internet message boards, and the government. Many CEOs have discovered how rude an awakening that can be. Which of these are you willing to trade away? Decide your currency before contacting investors; it will limit which investors you approach.

STEP 3. DECIDE WHAT YOU WANT TO BUY

Remember who is in charge of your company. For The Digital Pen, Anne was the buyer and the other party the supplier. As with any supplier, some have better products (in this case, resources) than others. As the buyer, what did Anne want to buy? She could buy money with her resources or some assets that are more valuable than money. These commodities could be worth more than cash.

Four Assets Worth More Than Cash

1. Skills
2. Market access
3. Less competition
4. Solution to an immediate problem

Do You Want to Buy Skills?

In a growing business, you will have to develop or buy skills. Before you look for investments, list the skills and tools that you want to get. A supplier that offers Web development skills would not be useful to Anne, but one that offers a sales channel or training for selling to large corporations might be. She is willing to pay more to buy that skill set.

Do You Want to Buy Market Access?

A partnership can buy access to markets. Entering into a partnership was a valuable lever for StrataCom, of San Jose, California. In critical growth periods, this supplier of network transmission and management products traded some control and information about future products to get access to markets controlled by DEC and Motorola. As time went on, the partnerships dissolved, leaving StrataCom behind as a strong market leader. Eventually, the company went full circle and bought market access by selling itself to Cisco Systems.

Do You Want to Buy Reduced Competition?

Sometimes the greatest throttle on margins is competition. By eliminating competition, your business can often gain control of margins. By merging with Chrysler, Daimler eliminated competitors. That lack of rivalry for customers may allow the succeeding company to maintain even higher margins on sport utility and alternative-fuel vehicles. If Anne planned a move into a potential competitor's turf, she might offer to sell the competitor some control in return for unimpeded access to the market.

Do You Want to Buy a Solution to an Immediate Problem?

Solving an immediate problem is the most common reason to look for resources. Most owners and managers looking for time, people, or money will do so as a reaction to an immediate threat. They desperately need a resource in order to survive or grow, and it shows in the negotiation. When your business is desperate is the worst time to go after resources.

Anne started her search for money as a way to avoid a cash-flow problem. Although her business was profitable, she wanted funds to stabilize it. The need felt urgent to her, and that pressure put her in a weak position. Angst does not improve cash flow. It could cost Anne control of her company in return for that cash.

What Anne Bought

As Anne worked through the issues, she realized that what she really wanted was to build her market access. She designed her box top around buying that access by giving up control and equity. She turned to her resource suppliers and asked what resources and access they would sell her. She made conscious decisions on what she wanted to buy with the control she was willing to give up and put herself in charge of the transaction. She turned a desperate and crazy-making situation into an opportunity for sustainable growth by treating the acquisition of resources like any other business transaction.

Despite being a graphically oriented person, Anne chose to describe her box top in words. The borders of the puzzle were:

- She, not others, would remain in control of the transaction.
- She would give up some control over the business as long as she could maintain certain activities.
- She would quickly get access to a larger market.
- She would get a piece of a larger profit opportunity.
- She could maintain family time at the level she had already chosen.

The box top caused Anne to eliminate several suppliers, and it saved her hundreds of hours in conversation and negotiation. It also saved her from accepting the first great offer, which was not the best for her.

Anne chose to merge with a company that had both market presence and competence in creating e-commerce tools above and beyond Web development. The skills of her team and those of the other company combined to make a whole greater than the sum of the parts. Anne got access to a much larger market. She set the stage for sustainable growth.

Stay Independent or Become a Division? Getting Resources

Anne chose to merge, but that might not be the correct decision for your business. For you, a better source of time, people, and money might come from staying independent. As you build a box top and search for more resources, consider what you must trade away to get them. The following subsections look at some trades and expectations you will deal with when weighing independent and corporate investors.

Why Sell Privately?

Taking private investors and selling the company are good alternatives when you want to gain resources other than cash. For instance, TCI sold itself to AT&T for strategic reasons. As a single company, it can do much more to combine networks than two independent companies could. Each management team wanted to enter the market the other dominated. Each team saw that neither company could quickly build the skills and investments required to compete effectively. They also calculated that government regulators would balk at allowing two companies to use cable access for new communications technologies but might allow a single entity to start up quickly. TCI also gained some cash, but the real advantage of the sale was the ability of a combined company to deliver integrated communications more quickly. This merger emphasized speed as much as money.

The same thinking applies to the acquisition of U.S. Robotics and Palm Computing by 3Com. Of course, 3Com could have entered the modem and handheld markets, and U.S. Robotics was quite capable of penetrating the network connection market. But why spend years building a market when you can buy it or be bought into it within months?

Money Has Strings—Concerns for Both Entrepreneurs and Intrapreneurs

Of the three resources, money may be the least important, but it gets the most attention. Money will never be free of restrictions. In a survey of executives who have been successful as both intrapreneurs and entrepreneurs, each made it clear that money always comes with strings attached.[2] Most general managers and owners believe otherwise. The independents assume that parent companies are generous with resources and are willing to invest them in growing businesses without restrictions. Divisional managers look at the independents and assume that they have it better. They know that getting the money is not hard: funding seems plentiful if you read the papers. However, getting the money without covenants is not likely. Venture capitalists (VCs), angels,[3] investment bankers, and corporations usually have specific expectations. These are detailed in the following subsections.

Growing a Division? Issues to Consider

In many ways, it's harder to grow a division than an independent company. One reason is that your time is not your own. You may be running a streamlined and no-frills operation, but the larger company may not. It may have two-day meetings to discuss wider issues and want you there. The company's accounting and control procedures will require your attention even if you have nothing to do with them. There will still be meetings for every manager at your level, and someone will always say, "Sure, invite her, too," without asking whether you want to go.

Your success as a subsidiary will make life harder. People who want to attach themselves to success populate every company. As you do well, they will ask for a piece of your time or want to add you to their distribution list. Then they will also ask whether you can include their product or idea in your business. The fact that your view of the business has nothing in common with their ideas does not stop them from trying. Instead, they will want the opportunity to tell you why you should change your view.

Politically, you want to say yes. These are people you want to keep on your side over the years. They have many worthwhile ideas. As a good corporate citizen, you'll go to meetings and be recognized. However, to grow sanely, consider two steps:

1. Move to a facility at least an hour away from headquarters. A time zone away is even better. You will travel more, but you will experience a net gain in time saved.

2. Learn to say no. Every time someone asks you to review a document, join a task force, attend a meeting of any size, or add a product line, you will have to respond. Your answer should be a question: "What damage will occur if I don't get to this issue before the next product launch?" Once in a great while, the requester will give you an excellent reason to do as he or she asks. Much more often, the answer will be weak and focused solely on the requester's own issues.

And no is very clearly the right thing to say. Time will always be your most expensive resource. You have fewer than eighty productive hours in an average workweek. Every time you take more than two or three of those for unproductive purposes, you are putting sustainable growth at risk.

Another reason that growing a division is hard is that the parent company will usually ask you to staff from within. At first, this seems like a perfect opportunity: you have access to people who come from a similar culture and understand how things are done in the larger corporation. They know how far they can push something and can often push an idea further because they know the players at the larger company.

But accepting those people can be like the worst nightmares from a cartoon Dilbert[4]. You can count on getting access to people who come with some baggage attached; the best people are rarely offered up. Some candidates will be great people who don't quite fit; some will have excellent personal reasons to move and a boss who is willing to help.

More often, the candidates others offer you will be people

who have not fit anywhere for a long time. Their bosses will suggest that what they really need is a chance to act as entrepreneurs. That may be true, or it may be that they really need a new company. Even so, your responsibility is to your charter and not to the candidates or their managers. In order to grow sanely, you will need to make two rules clear from the first conversations you have about recruiting:

1. You only take people who *you* are comfortable will fit into the intrapreneurial culture that you are developing.

2. If you don't feel completely satisfied with the fit, you reserve the right to refuse—no matter how good they may be and no matter who knows whom or needs what. You have a start-up here. You need the ability to decide whom you will have involved.

Watch for one serious limit to every corporate/internal start-up combination—the agenda of the parent. When a company creates a start-up, it has a reason. That reason may have nothing to do with your reason to be running the division. If you do not understand that difference, you will quickly run up against conflicts.

This agenda issue can involve something as simple as the targets of the division. If you are there to make a profit and the sponsors are looking for revenue or market share, that conflict will be critical. If you want to expand but the corporation wants you to stay in one market, you are going to have to deal with frustration. As I discuss later in this chapter, the time, people, and money you receive come bundled with expectations.

Growing an Independent Business? Issues to Consider

In many ways, growing an independent company is harder than growing a division of a larger company. (See Table 5-1.)

One overriding concern is that your time is not your own. Your customers, employees, suppliers, contractors and consultants, and investors will all want to talk to you. If you are successful at growing well, so will outsiders, such as the media, business schools, community groups, and deserving charities.

When you add these up, your eighty-hour week will only have forty productive hours in it—and you still don't get to see your family.

The only reasonable answer is to say no. Then you must rank your time commitments so that you can live with them. If you decide that your customers are more deserving of time than investors, you have to live with that. Make these decisions using jigsaw management, and let everyone know your box top. Become known as the business owner who has set his or her priorities and lives with them.

"No" sometimes applies to people who want to work for your team. Not all employees work well in independent companies. Many people who think that they want to work in a fast-growing company really don't. They aren't dishonest; they just don't know any better.

Because successful fast-growth companies are the minority, most candidates who come to you will have no real experience with these pressures. They won't know that they lack that experience until it becomes a problem for both of you. You can't rely on outside recruiters, because they usually don't have any experience with successful growth either. The only person who can help sort this out is the hiring manager.

CORPORATE INVESTORS VS. VENTURE CAPITALISTS

The decision to take investors might come when you are starting up, or you could face it later when you want more resources to fuel entry into a new market. Perhaps you and your fellow founders only want more personal time or money. You have a choice of how to get those resources.

One option is to go to the venture capital community or investment banking community and ask for a cash investment. A second option is to go to a corporation and ask that it take a stake in, or even buy, your company. Private investors and corporations will each approach a deal with different expectations, and your choice should allow for those expectations. Before you approach either group, make sure you understand what its expectations are. The next two subsections summarize the expectations you should take into account.[5]

What Do VCs and Investment Bankers Expect from You for Their Investment?

Venture capitalists and investment bankers are not just for entrepreneurial start-ups. Many established companies work with them to move a division from intrapreneurial status to partly or fully independent companies. As an example, Loewe New Media spun some people and technology off into a new venture that became ZADU. Loewe used VCs and angels to supply the financing while it kept a minority position, looking for a long-term return.

How Important Are Quick Returns?

When you go to VCs and investment bankers (I will call both VCs for the rest of this section), you will have to deal with the specific expectations that they have. Although each company will have a different spin on this, you can assume that it expects a quick return on its money. Plan on meeting your commitments to deliver that return. It may be tempting to agree to whatever dates are suggested just to get the deal done, but with a good VC, that will be a mistake. If you plan well and meet your goals, most venture capitalists and bankers will leave you alone to grow. However, unlike many corporations, a prudent VC will take action when you miss a commitment—and you might not like that action.

The Value of Products

VCs don't have the same love of technology that you might. Many VCs are willing to sacrifice the product when it seems appropriate. To a good VC, the product is less important than the people. Which market you want to enter is less important than ensuring that the market will be there. Scott Kriens, CEO of fast-growing Juniper Networks, observed that the product is less important to VCs than the team and the market's ability to support a product:

There are two pressures from a good venture capitalist: one is the team; the other is market size. These are
the pivot points that any deal will hang on. Without
the right team, [even the best] idea will crater. Even if
you do not have a great idea, if you have the right
market proposition and a smart team, whether the
product is exactly right or not, they will fix that.[6]

This does not mean that a VC will stay out of your day-to-
day operations. As Kriens notes, "If the business is going well,
the VCs tend to stay pretty passive. If not, they ask a lot of questions that a good management team would already be asking.
They tend to get into a lot of the operating details."

How Much Growth Is Not Enough?

How much growth you achieve is also an expectations
issue. Kevin Kerns, of Apropos Technologies, comments that
with VCs[7]:

There are great demands for ramp and delivery, more
than you would get typically inside a corporation. As
a subsidiary, if you grow 30 percent a year and the
parent grows 15 percent, you are a hero. With a VC, if
you are not growing 150 percent, you are not cutting
it. VCs compare their investment against other companies in the same marketplace. Parent companies compare you to other things the parent is doing.

No one can tell you exactly how much growth is enough.
However, no matter what rate seems correct to you, it must also
meet the expectations of your VC.

Markets and Infrastructure

Venture capitalists bring more than money: they bring contacts and respectability. If a VC invests in your growth, it be-
hooves the company to support you with contacts and
connections. Involving a well-connected VC will make other
people more willing to help you.

That support does not translate into infrastructure; VCs will expect you to build your own independent support systems. Doing so is a substantial distraction. Installing a new accounting system or leasing real estate consumes time that you could otherwise invest in growth. If you want to avoid this hassle, consider looking for corporate sponsorship.

Investing Resources to Get Resources

The comparative surplus of funds among VCs is a disadvantage to you in one key sense. Each company's partners expect you to pitch a convincing story as *they* see it. The time required to build the pitch is a considerable investment. To research for, prepare, and deliver a one-hour request for funds can take weeks, and every hour you spend on this effort is an hour lost to growing the company.

What Do Corporations Expect From You for Their Investment?

Corporations also have specific expectations. Each will be at least a little different, but they all share some common expectations that you will need to consider. Those expectations may be exactly wrong for your company and personal goals; you could get the resources and hate the restrictions. These conflicts are summarized in Table 5-1 and detailed in the following subsections.

How Important Are Quick Returns?

Unlike VCs, corporations may not expect or even want a quick return on cash. Even when they do want that payout, larger companies are more likely than private investors to let the committed return slide a quarter or two. They often value other assets, such as access to a new technology or market. Sometimes they will invest in you as a defensive maneuver, to keep one of their competitors from getting that access or to chill a market. These subjective reasons can be a better fit for some growing companies than an investor who wants quick access to cash.

For instance, if you want to dominate a market more quickly, you can do so by letting a larger corporation acquire

Table 5-1. Conflicting goals.

Goals in Starting Intrapreneurial Business	Conflicts with Goals of Investors
Open a new market	Profitability and growth are subordinate to learning and creating presence. Some companies create Internet divisions so that they can play in that market. Others do so to make as much money as possible. The two do not coexist well.
Open a new territory	Entering new geography has high start-up costs. Companies do it for strategic reasons. If short-term financial goals exist, they are at risk.
Generate a great deal of cash by going partly public	With hot equity markets, some corporations create divisions that they can take public in order to get cash. Because the markets value growth, market protection or profit goals may interfere.
Protect a market	Market share often conflicts with profits or products. If customers might leave in order to get access to something, the company may provide that product or service even if it means losing money.
Introduce a new product line	Product strategy may be owned by HQ, and local product innovation may not be supported. Divisional growth and profits are sacrificed for larger strategy goals.
Any one or two of the five goals can coexist. All five cannot.	

you. Consider Norstan Corporation's decision to sell one of its most profitable businesses to a larger company.[8] The company's Previously Owned Equipment (POE) division was a major player in the market for used ROLM Computerized Branch Exchanges (CBXs). Even so, Norstan only had 20 percent of the market. Norstan could have grown that market without help, but the company chose to speed up that growth. Norstan sold its operations to ROLM, which put POE at the top of the market.

Selling behind ROLM's name and through ROLM's sales force allowed POE to take more than 50 percent of the market in a matter of months. ROLM was not looking for a quick financial return from this. If the return had been delayed by two quarters, ROLM would almost certainly have forgiven the unit's managers. The value to ROLM was in being in the market.

The corporation's willingness to alter financial goals can also work against you. If the political landscape inside your investor's corporation changes, you might find that someone suddenly changes your targets for you. As an example, when I was running an intrapreneurial division in the 1990s, the company moved the reporting chain from an executive with a marketing focus to one with sales responsibility. The new executive changed the targets of my division from profit to revenue in the last quarter of the fiscal year. Decisions that we had made months before were suddenly wrong. The resources required to make that change were difficult to acquire. A quick decision by a new corporate executive cost the division staff a great deal of time and energy.

Consistency is not the hallmark of most corporations, and sudden changes like that one will interfere with sustainable growth. Such a change would be rare with a VC, but as a corporate division, you will always be vulnerable to quick alterations that do not make sense for your business. Other people's agendas will often control yours.

The goals and priorities of corporate investors may change more frequently than you would prefer. If you sell to or take an investment from a corporation, you should expect to invest time in selling and then reselling your priorities to the management team.

The Value of Products

Unlike VCs, expect corporations to care a great deal about the product and the specific market you are entering. A product that tightly complements the corporation's mix is highly desirable. A product that does not relate in any way to the corporate investor's products may get starved by lack of resources. A product that competes with the corporation is a candidate for quick death.

In the same way, a corporate investor will pay more to enter or hold markets that are strategically important. If your growth can help the corporation enter those markets or improve its standing there, your value is higher. You will have an easier time getting the resources you need to grow. However, if your growth will be exceptional but you don't do much for the wider corporate agenda, expect less support.

Demands on Time

The freedom to set your own agenda represents a difference that might matter on a personal level. Whereas a good VC will stay out of your successful business, you can expect the opposite from a corporate investor. The more you grow successfully, the more you can expect people across the corporation to tag projects onto your work. People will ask you to work on task forces, and you will be attending meetings that have nothing to do with you. Managers will request your opinion on issues that have little relevance to your skills. Others will assign projects to you because you can get things done—regardless of whether you have the time or skill available. You should expect to have to fend off these demands in order to stay focused and maintain sustainable growth.

How Much Growth Is Too Much?

The discussion of expectations also includes issues as basic as the definition of "enough" growth. As Kevin Kerns of Apropos notes, corporate investors will usually compare your growth against their own. Because that will probably be less than yours, you have an edge. On the other hand, if the corporate investors grow their business at 15 percent per year, you may find that they don't see a need to help your business achieve 120 percent growth in the same period. You may have to repeatedly sell the need for triple-digit growth.

Markets and Infrastructure

Corporations can bring you more than money. They can also provide access to internal resources and market presence. Access to sophisticated research and development can be a wonderful advantage. Having the name of a respected investor on your side can be a real support when you enter a new market.

This can translate into infrastructure and be an advantage when time is at a premium. Instead of shopping for space or an accounting system, you may be able to borrow the investor corporation's infrastructure. Of course, if the infrastructure is needlessly elegant or complicated, any time savings is not going to last. Implementing the corporation's enterprise resource planning package might take much more effort than installing a simpler accounting system.

CAN YOU DO BOTH?

Most entrepreneurs look at corporations as behemoths that demand total ownership. That view is no longer appropriate. If you are growing rapidly and want resources, you can approach corporations for small investments as well as a complete takeover. As mentioned earlier in the chapter, StrataCom[9] did both. Early in its spectacular growth, the network products company asked several large corporations to invest cash. In return, Motorola, Digital Equipment, and others got:

- Better access to information on a new technology
- Better chance to understand a new market
- Early knowledge of market moves and changes
- Opportunity (through board seats) to influence a dominant player in that market

The corporations invested tens of millions of dollars. Although it was not expensive to the investors, that money was an important tool for fueling StrataCom's growth.

Staying Internal

Unlike StrataCom, Pitney Bowes's Internet-based postage meter division was treated as a wholly owned intrapreneurial start-up from the beginning. The division took resources only from the parent company and chose to market its product under the Pitney Bowes label. This eliminated the diversion of looking for investors and sponsors.

It also had a chilling effect on competitors. Your business will need to allocate more time and money to compete with a known leader than it would to compete with an independent start-up. Companies that would consider investing in the Internet postage-meter business might decide that competing with Pitney Bowes's market clout and ability to sue for patent protection would make the business more difficult than it would be worth.[10]

The Most Important Expectation

Outside investors and investor companies always have one expectation in common. Ted Antonitis, CEO of ONEAC, observes, "No one will tolerate surprise."[11] Impatience, in turn, leads to the loss of additional time—time the business could use to build sustainable growth.

Any growing company will need resources. Scrambling to get them can be crazy-making. Or you can set a box top and look for the best investor, one that brings you the right combination of skills, market, and resources. The choice will be the investor's if you wait until you need the resources. The choice of the best investor will be yours if you plan to take control of the process.

Notes

1. Anne and the company are real, but their names have been changed.
2. Survey by The Meyer Group (1999).

3. Angels are small private investors, usually individuals, who will put personal funds into a promising growth opportunity. The investments are usually smaller than the amounts VCs will invest but easier to get.
4. Dilbert, by cartoonist Scott Adams, © United Feature Syndicate.
5. In 1998, The Meyer Group did a survey of executives who had gone both routes. This section is a summary of some of their most useful experiences.
6. Personal conversation with the author (1999).
7. Personal conversation with the author (1999).
8. The Norstan/ROLM story is based on the author's personal experiences.
9. StrataCom was a networking technology company in San Jose, California. In a few years, it grew from a start-up to the two transactions described here, the second of which occurred in 1996.
10. For more on Pitney Bowes, patent suits, and smaller Internet competition, see "Patent War Pending," *San Jose Mercury News,* July 18, 1999.
11. Personal conversation with the author (1998).

PART TWO

Resource Strategies and Applications

CHAPTER SIX

Resource Strategies: Grow and Dominate New Markets

Your business will always have the new-market choice: should you excel in an existing market or try to create and then dominate a new one? Neither task is easy; each will put great stress on your business's resources.

When you decide to invest time, people, and money in an existing market, you are competing with others who have their own, often substantial, advantages. To succeed, you will have to execute with great skill and in precise time frames. If you want to beat others to market acceptance, your business will need money, people, and especially the ability to manage time. If you can't beat others to market acceptance, you will find yourself in a price war. Then your ability to manage minute costs will be a key differentiator. Operational excellence is hard, and for the winner, it can be rewarding.

New markets, however, are different.

CREATING AND DOMINATING MARKETS—THE OWNER'S OR GM'S ROLE

In Chapter 3, I discussed why successful CEOs focus on new markets and why these markets are valuable to sustainable growth. In this chapter and the next, I discuss how to invest in them in the most intelligent way. This chapter discusses the overall strategy and offers some practical suggestions.[1] The next chapter looks at some key applications. Again, in the space I have, I will not be able to cover all the applications you might wish to use. However, I can cover some of the more interesting ones. (See Chart 6-1).

Growing in existing markets requires excellent operational skills in marketing, sales, development, and other areas. New markets require that you add another skill to operational excellence. Not only must you choose the right market; you must also guide your resources to work where they have never been. Both are skills the owner or general manager must wield.

The Attraction of New Markets

Maintaining a profit in today's markets is not easy. The barriers that might keep others out of your market never seem high enough. Competitive activity constantly drives your marketing costs up and operating margins down. A way out of the crunch is to create and dominate a new market, one where your business faces no competitive pressures. New markets are the holy grail for many executives, in both established companies and start-ups.

At first, it seems easy. After all, you might ask, if all these thirty-year-old technical wizards can have an idea and then dominate a new market, why can't you? And once you do, like Microsoft with Windows and Glaxo Wellcome with AZT, you can maintain a healthy profit. Another part of the attraction is the idea of changing the rules. Geoff Bezos started a bookstore without a physical retail shop. Amazon.com created and dominates a new market. Mirabilis created an Internet product and gave it away free. America Online paid more than a quarter billion dollars for Mirabilis before the smaller company ever gained revenue. Doing things that seem impossible to others can be very satisfying.

The problem is that creating and dominating a market is far from easy. For every Amazon.com, there is a Pointcast (discussed later in this chapter). To succeed, the general executive has to look where most functional managers are unwilling and untrained to look. Then you have to guide your team to ask the right questions, some of which are shown in Figure 6-1 and discussed in the following section.

Chart 6-1. Platform chart for sustainable warp-speed growth.

	Chapter 12	Warp-Speed Growth: Managing a Business Built for Speed							
	Chapters 7, 9, 11	APPLICATIONS ☛	Pricing	Tailoring	Prospective rewards	Indies	Prospective appraisals	Killer apps	Pain
	Chapters 6, 8, 10	INVESTMENT STRATEGY ☛	Strategy—new markets		Strategy—recruiting and structure			Strategy—effect before technology (change is bad)	
	Chapters 1–5	WHAT TO INVEST ☛	Time		People			Money	
		WHERE TO INVEST ☛	Create, dominate new markets		Technology			People	
		FOUNDATION ☛	Jigsaw management—Building a box top Deciding and communicating what to work on and what to let go						

New Markets Are Hard

It's easy to think of ways to extend a product into an existing market—and harder to make it work. You need operational skill

Figure 6-1. Questions for an owner or a GM to ask.

As you look at the opportunity and risk from new markets, here are some key questions to ask. Ask the users, ask your team, and ask yourself.

To the users:

—If you could do this, would you get really excited? What *would* get you really excited?

—What problems keep you up at night?

To your team and you:

—Are we solving a real problem, or do we have a solution in search of a problem?

—What do we have to do to be first to market acceptance?

—What are our customers doing in today's market that we never expected? Can we see a new market from that?

—Is the inherent value there for the buyers or for a third party? Who should be paying for this?

—Can we identify a channel that will get that value to the buyers very quickly and efficiently?

—Can we establish a good relationship directly with the buyers no matter which channel we use?

To you:

—Does your instinct support your analytical decision to try and create the market?

—Are you watching your sales team for unexpected markets?

at many functions to get the right results. Consider the effort to develop a new version of a digital cell phone. Success will require high-quality work from each of your engineering, manufacturing, marketing, sales, and financial teams. Creating a great product puts you into a highly competitive market. That market will reward your ability to choose the right distribution channel and to offer a little more value at a lower cost. These forms of operational excellence require superb functional skills. They are also tasks that the CEO is usually willing to delegate. Rose Rambo, vice president and general manager at Polycom, notes, "Product line extensions fund the new markets, but can't become them."[2]

New markets are different. Here, cost is less of an issue than finding the combination of channel, features, and abilities that is so attractive that it will create a new market and allow you to dominate it. This combination is the "killer application."

Two paths can do this. Path 1 is to extend into a previously unthought-of market. Path 2 is to extend a proven product into a market that is known but has never been tapped.

Netscape's history provides an example of path 1. Before it started, Internet browsers were free but low-quality. No cohesive market existed. Netscape broke a few rules (for example, the company gave its product away to create the market; it delivered unfinished products to users as part of the testing cycle) and then used a close connection with the product's advanced users to create and dominate a new market.

Edwin Land did the same thing with his instant camera. He had a new idea that broke a few rules (asking the user to participate in developing the film was a significant risk) and created a new market. Polaroid dominated that market for decades, successfully keeping competitors out. Whereas Netscape used speed and closeness with users to create a barrier against entry, Polaroid used patents and aggressive marketing to make its product name synonymous with instant photography.

However, not all new markets require new products. You can take a good product to a known but untapped market. Sometimes it's only a question of finding a new group of users or a new geography. This is path 2.

AZT was created thirty years ago as a cancer treatment, a market in which it did not sell well. Twenty years later, Burroughs Wellcome (which later became Glaxo Wellcome) found a new market, patients with acquired immune deficiency syndrome (AIDS), and moved the product to that new market.

Figure 6-2. Two paths to new markets.

Today, AZT is the standard for use in most initial HIV treatment plans.

Cell phones provide another example of this path. Although Motorola was planning to enter existing analog markets with digital cell phones, the company also aimed to enter markets that never had any cell phones. After all, some company had to be the first cell phone provider in China.

Entering a new cell phone market in another country involves great risk. You don't know that the users will actually accept the idea of wireless. Your business will have to make large investments to adapt your technology and modify the systems so that they will work with the local voltages and dial tones. Your team will have serious political and regulatory issues to resolve. The considerable resources that you must dedicate to a single geography might be better used for other projects. You have high opportunity costs when you invest time, people, and money in that new country.

Simultaneously, you will have tremendous upside. Not only can you become the dominant supplier of phones, but you can supply the infrastructure to make those handsets work. Someone has to sell all those towers and switches. Why not you? A cell phone supplier could dominate whole countries by a combination of political and business agreements.

Here, the new market is defined not by product but by previous availability. You may have done as well as practical in a saturated market while a parallel market has not yet been touched. As Glaxo Wellcome has done with AZT and Motorola with cell phone systems, you, too, can look at new, parallel markets for your key products.

Of course, there is another path—taking an unproven product to an unproven market. That is not a good choice for executives with limited ability to lose it all. A wiser decision will be to take one path and build a box top around it.

Investing Your Resources

Whether you have an existing business or a new one, your resources are going to be spread thin when the time comes to invest in new markets. Time is the most important resource, but not time to market. That makes little difference in creating new markets. The rewards for being the first company to achieve market *acceptance* are much higher than for simply being the company to deliver first.

Today, Microsoft dominates the market for PC office software suites over WordPerfect/Corel and Lotus/IBM. It might have been different. WordPerfect was the dominant supplier of word-processing software in the DOS market into 1990 and 1991. The company was so dominant that neither Microsoft (Word) nor IBM (DisplayWrite) could use its significant market presence to make an inroad. As first to market *acceptance*, Word-Perfect had won that contest.

However, no word-processing software worked well in the new Windows operating system, and Windows was becoming more popular. Both WordPerfect and IBM were slow to bring a Windows product to acceptance. Microsoft delivered software that got that market acceptance. Today, Microsoft controls more than three-fourths of the market. Again, the first to achieve market acceptance was the victor. Time to market is less important than time to market acceptance.

Acceptance by the media and influencers (consultants and analysts) is important but not enough to make the product successful. Acceptance by the users must come first. In the race to provide the first working protease inhibitor combination for HIV patients, saquinavir was first to market. However, Merck used a quirk in the approval process to help Crixivan become more acceptable to patients. Today, Crixivan is the dominant drug.

The worst case is the one in which you gain the acceptance of the wrong people. Like other companies developing Internet push technology, Pointcast earned acceptance from almost everyone but the users. The result was a highly touted company that has yet to succeed.

Time to Market vs. Market Acceptance

Being first does not always mean success. One of the most highly touted firsts in the Internet world was push technology. However, the company that established itself as the standard for the market could not convert that market presence into economic success.

Push technology is a tool that allows users to choose what they would like to get from the World Wide Web and have it continually delivered to them. Users just sign on, and the information they have selected flows across their computer screens while they are not actively doing something else. Advertisers pay the cost. They get the opportunity to "buy eyeballs" who they hope will see their message. The market definer and leader has been Pointcast, in Sunnyvale, California.

Pointcast was successful in defining and dominating the market. It signed up a quarter million new users per month for a period, making the company a major success in delivering eyeballs to advertisers. Pointcast grew in clout and perceived value. In 1996, less than two years after it shipped its first product, the company was rumored to be negotiating its own sale to News Corp. for $450 million. Not bad for a company with a product it gave away at no cost.

Unfortunately for the company and the advertisers, users got little benefit. They got updates on the news, but those updates turned out to be less important to them than the reliability problems that many experienced. Users turned sour on the product. Many information services departments started to limit Pointcast on corporate networks so that they could save network capacity for the business. The users did not care enough to want Pointcast's service. Advertisers could no longer count on a return. The economic equation started to fail. In 1999, Pointcast announced that another company would acquire it at a small percentage of the 1996 value.

It was a great idea, but it failed. Don't let the romance of the product blind you to the need to make the investments necessary to create a great user experience. The CEO or general manager has the responsibility of ensuring that the target market sees the value.

Guiding People

After time, the second key resource for a rapidly growing company is people. Pointing them in the right direction is the task of the owner or general manager. Not only must you choose where to open a market; you must guide your resources to work where they have never been. The CEO or general manager must wield this skill. Businesses equip most functions poorly to help you gain quick acceptance in new markets.

Your marketing team can help to define what will sell to existing customers and how the product should look to a defined market. The problem comes in uncovering new markets. Modern marketing provides less help there. Customers often have no idea that they make up a new market. As an example, suppliers priced the first fax machines at around a thousand dollars each, marketed toward a limited set of customers. Participants in the market that eventually evolved (small businesses, departments, and home offices) continually said that they did not see a need for the product and would not spend the money required to buy early fax machines. Marketing teams listened to the customers and focused the product and the pitch on the high end. They did what they are supposed to do.

Someone else broke that set of marketing rules, choosing to enter with a low-cost solution even if the customers did not know they wanted a fax. Traditional marketing would never have predicted the success of the fax. Business as usual is not much help at finding truly new markets.

Your sales team is another important resource that cannot lead the effort. To compete successfully, you will need to dedicate your best salespeople to known markets. Diverting these specialists into other areas, even for a short while, puts your existing revenue stream at risk.[3] Even so, your salespeople and channels still play a role in creating new markets. They can accidentally explore new markets for you.

Occasionally, someone will ignore the rules and find a new place to sell your products. For example, if some doctors take your pharmaceuticals off label (use them for another treatment), find out how and why. You may have a new AZT. Twenty years ago, a salesperson changed the orientation of an entire telephone system (PBX) company by consistently selling to a market that was not supposed to buy—universities. Instead of trying to enforce rules firmly, you can watch for these exceptions and use them to your advantage. Attempts to go outside the market are like mutations; they rarely work. However, there is always one that may become a billion-dollar product like AZT. Make sure you can spot that exception when it happens.

When it comes time to choose a new market to enter, the entire team should be involved. You can and should ask some specific questions (shown earlier in Figure 6-1), but all you'll get are partial answers. Marketing, sales, or finance cannot make the final decision. That choice rests with the owner or general manager.

The decision comes down to this:

* Are you solving a problem that people will resonate with, such as getting a word processor that can be used with Windows?

or

* Do you have a solution in search of a problem, such as push technology?

The new market becomes a gut call, which is the province of the owner or general manager. You have to ask the right questions, determine whether you can get to market acceptance, and then make the call.

PRICING TO CREATE AND DOMINATE MARKETS

When you decide to grow by creating and dominating a market, pricing becomes one of your key tools. For many growing businesses, pricing is a mathematical decision: price equals costs plus overhead plus profit. But it can also help your business create new markets that you can then dominate. When you do this, pricing becomes much more important than merely covering your costs.

Pricing for New Markets—Internal and External Views

When you plan to define the market from scratch, pricing is a key early decision. Here, you have two views to consider—one internal, the other external. In the internal view of pricing, you assess the cost of materials and how to spread the fixed and variable costs of your business. Ideally, you price so that you achieve a profit without sacrificing volumes. This process is internally focused, defined by the needs of your business and your strategies. (See Figure 6-3.)

In the external view, your price is a tool to define your market. When you price at one point, you may find that you will compete in the existing market. Setting your price at a significantly higher or lower level may create a market where none existed before. As paradoxical as it may seem, a higher price may make you more competitive. Let's explore this.

Looking internally, when you decide to compete in an existing market, your costs are a key component of your plan. You will need operational excellence to keep costs low and margins acceptable. For example, if you choose to enter the market for over-the-counter painkillers, your ability to stay within a certain price range is critical to working with distributors. The good news is that you know the price point before you start. The expectations are set.

In existing markets, you can know and then balance the expectations, the cost of doing business, and your forecast for volumes. That balance gives you stability and allows you to identify a break-even point.

The balance fails when you want to create and dominate a new market. In an unknown market, you can't price by expectations. You have no knowledge of a working price point. That means that volume forecasts resemble fiction more than fact. Without dependable volume forecasts, you can't even determine the costs of doing business.

If you decide to develop a new over-the-counter medication, you know that your costs will be substantial. What you do not know is whether anyone will buy it. If you decide to offer a new kind of service as a consultant, you can put your costs in a spreadsheet. However, you can't know whether the service will sell. Volume forecasting is futile. Your internal view of pricing is so incomplete that it will be of little value. When you enter that painkiller market, existing dynamics have already set price expectations. The dynamic is reversed in a new market, because customers have no expectations. Instead, *a new market defines price expectations.*

So for creating and dominating a new market, look externally. In the external view, price depends on larger goals. These might include creating stock value, attracting a certain market, or making it easy to acquire your first product so you can sell a second.

If your goal is to increase stock value, you might price to create a new market without regard to costs. This has certainly worked for others. In the 1990s, the market values of Amazon. com, @Home, and America Online didn't seem related to their operating margins. Instead, the valuations seemed to relate to how much these market creators and dominators can grow.

In creating new markets, your price can be a tool to attract the right customers. Looking at your prices early should cause you to choose target customers before you choose a profit level. The key to success is knowing your target customers. If your target market is likely to respond at a set price point, your best chance of success comes when you meet that point. If that point is lower than your costs, you have an operational challenge, the same one many Internet companies face: you have to deliver something at that price point and still have money to operate.

But what if the best buying response comes at a higher price point? Should you reduce your ability to reach the market so that you can lower the price and make less money? Perhaps you would be better off making more money and attracting exactly the customers you wish even if your profit feels too high. Pros-

Figure 6-3. Internal vs. external view of pricing.

Internal View	External View
—Price to profit	—Price to market
—Cost-based pricing	—Price to market
—Explicit expectations set	—No known expectations
—Forecasting volumes important	—Forecasting volumes ineffective
—Stock market value important	—Stock market value important
—Goal is to build profit.	—Profit sacrificed to stock market value

pects in a new market may drive you to enter at a *higher* price point than you had planned.

Pricing as a Marketing Tool

Many people will not buy a superior product at a very low price. The buyer of a notebook computer enters the market with a pre-conceived idea of what he or she will spend. A client will have a clear idea of what consulting is worth per hour—no matter who provides it. When a family decides to buy a luxury car, they expect a certain price range.

A price point represents a comfort zone. Customers will compare it with the results they expect from the product or service. This makes comfort a part of the sales and pricing strategy. Let me suggest a real case example involving services.

A business strategy consultant in California, Jean Mays uses price to define her market. One prospect, BigTel, needed critical analysis done before an intrapreneurial business launch.[4] Because it was a high-profile launch, many executives were involved in the decisions. As with most internal start-ups, they ran this new business in accordance with many of the rules and habits of the parent company.

One of those comfortable habits was to spend $400 per hour for consulting. BigTel considered several consultants for the work. Of those, Jean was the highest-priced, at twice the cost of the next highest-priced consultant. Jean feels that that helped her win the deal.

She did a good job, but was it twice as good as the next highest-priced consultant would have done? Probably not. However, the parent company saw real value in using a consultant who fit its way of doing business. Another consultant might have delivered the same ideas at a lower cost. The question, however, is whether BigTel would have accepted those ideas. Just because it paid less for them, BigTel's executives might not have been comfortable with the suggestions. Customers commonly discount the quality of a product when you discount the price. Although Jean's price was considerably higher than what other consultants charged, it was within the price range BigTel was comfortable paying. Comfort is important in choosing a consultant. Jean uses pricing to make her a more comfortable choice.

That comfort is even more important in a new market. With no habit or social guidelines to follow, a customer will be more likely to say no to something vaguely disquieting. It's easier to sell something at a comfortable price, even if that price is higher.

A price point also represents an image that the customer may wish to project. It feeds into the self-image that every company, client, and customer has. If the family selects a Lexus, it still has a choice of dealers. If one dealer offers a new car at $42,000 and the next dealer offers the same car at $24,000, most families will choose the more expensive car.

Why? First, to feel safe. Most people will wonder what is wrong with the lower-priced car. Second, customers make some decisions on the basis of status, and price is part of that. Driving a Lexus enhances the owner's prestige. Hiring the services of a famous architect does the same for a company's new headquarters. It infers that the owner or the company can afford the best. Exclusivity brings a sense of value. In a new market, a high price can enhance that sense of uniqueness.

Customers also link pricing to the perceived economic value of the problem to be solved. The more serious the issue, the more people expect to pay for a solution. It's a rational response. If you have a business problem that keeps you up at night, you want to believe that the vendor helping you will understand how difficult or important the problem is.

What Price in a New Market Can Suggest

- ❖ Comfort
- ❖ Prestige
- ❖ Exclusivity
- ❖ Higher-quality solutions

Pricing to Market—Example Applications

Consider the cost of replacing your existing computers with an entirely new concept such as network computers (see Chapter 11). You get substantial value from your installed technology, so you'd want to make sure that any new solution would offer results that are at least as good, if not better. Most customers expect to pay accordingly. If someone offered you a new concept priced at around $3,000 per workstation, you would probably consider it. If someone else came to you and offered you the same results for $300, would you wonder what the catch is? For most customers, it all sounds too good to be true. People expect to pay for quality and look askance at something that seems too inexpensive. Paradoxically, if network computers had cost $1,800 per workstation, they might have been more acceptable.

Merck had a similar issue to consider when it discovered that finasteride not only reduced the size of some enlarged prostates; it reversed male-pattern baldness in many men.[5] Merck was already selling the compound as Proscar for approximately $65 per month to insurers and health-care providers. The patient paid $13 to $16 a month.

In 1998, no real market for pharmaceutical baldness pills existed. Merck looked at the products available and decided, "You will find all kinds of schlock, potions, and lotions that cost $50, $60, $70 a month that don't do anything."[6] Merck could have entered the market at the same price per gram as Proscar, $13 to $16 per month to the patient. Instead, the company chose to define a new market—customers who would buy pill treatments for male-pattern baldness but only from major pharmaceutical suppliers. Merck offered the same product as Propecia and at a substantially higher price: approximately $45 to $50. In effect, consumers could buy the same finasteride for two different prices.

Male-pattern baldness is a substantial issue for many men, one they take very seriously. It would be fair to assume that they are willing to pay an accordingly serious amount for an effective solution. Would they put the same faith in a $10 treatment as they would put in a treatment five times as expensive? Would they be as likely to use it religiously if it were the same price as a fast-food meal? The answer appears to clearly be no.

These are exceptions; they show a smart use of pricing. The more common pricing strategies emulate network computers. They try to enter at the lowest possible price point, hoping to capture as many buyers as they can. Many entrepreneurs imagine that because giving the product away helped create a new market for Netscape, it can do the same for anyone. Building a plan on that assumption would be a mistake.

Can a Low Price Put You at Risk?

Setting a high price can produce three counterintuitive effects in the market:

1. *A higher price may be more attractive.* This might seem odd, but consider the case of Larry K., an entrepreneur in Virginia. Opening a new seminars market, he priced his programs very attractively. Even so, attendance was below breakeven. Then he tripled his price for the same offering. Attendance increased by 250 percent. Buyers saw more value at that higher price and responded accordingly. The product did not change, just the price.

2. *Some customers want to be sure you understand.* At a higher price, you may appeal to the customer who wants you to understand how difficult or important the problem is. If you charge $100,000 for a problem that he or she thinks is going to cost $250,000 to fix, the customer may wonder whether you have underestimated the issues. One experience of direct marketing is that volumes may go *up* when you raise a price. Your price can be too low and cost you sales because your customer is not comfortable that the product or service will really work.

3. *Usage is linked to price.* When people or companies pay a substantial amount for something, they are more likely to use it. Correctly or not, customers equate value with price. If the price is low, usage can suffer. You might wind up shipping large volumes without getting the usage you want. When usage drops, so does word of mouth. Repeat sales dry up. A low price can put you at risk in new markets.

A Pricing Process for Creating New Markets

Let's examine a process that you can use to set a price that will help you create and dominate a new market. First, we'll look at the steps in the process and then consider an example of how to use it. To start, reverse your normal inclinations with regard to pricing. Instead of pricing to cost and pricing as low as possible, follow these four steps:

1. Decide who makes up your market. The key is to narrow the definition of your primary target customers.
2. Estimate how much economic value they will get from your work.
3. Estimate what that set of customers would regard as a comfortable price.
4. Guess where the break-even would be at that price. Use that to define your exit strategy.

As an example, you might apply the four steps in the following way to create a new market for a painkiller:

1. If your market includes patients who suffer from migraine headaches, that eliminates the classic pain market. Normal headaches, sprains, even broken bones are outside your market. Focus only on the people who have migraines. Migraines are a problem that sufferers feel deeply and will pay dearly to solve. You can also quickly see that your market is individuals, not HMOs or health plans. Migraines are a pain that people will pay out of their own pockets to alleviate.

2. The economic value of your solution is high. It would not take long to determine that migraines cost hundreds of thousands or even millions of workdays per year. On an individual level, you can survey migraine sufferers to determine how much impact the pain has on their ability to earn money.

3. Surveys and conversations can also tell you what a comfortable price would be, for that set of customers. You would quickly find out that the price has a floor and a ceiling. A person suffering from a migraine headache may be willing to pay $10.00 to $15.00 per incident to relieve that pain. Would he or she trust a pill that claimed to provide pain relief for less than $2.50 per incident?

4. After the cost of patents, development, licensing, and approval, you may have invested millions of dollars to get to the

point of being able to manufacture the drug. Even then, you may not know the drug's real market potential. However, you can build a formula that will show you how many prescriptions you need to sell at $120 per package of ten to break even. As you enter the market and it responds, revisit your calculations. You can decide when to consider scaling the price down to raise the barrier to competition, as Hewlett-Packard has done with printers. There are other exit strategies. Choose one early. Changing your exit strategy is easier than starting the process as profits die off.

Price setting can be either an art or a science. Although you can jump in and start setting prices without thinking about your environment, your chances of achieving that elusive success increase when you use price to choose your customer set. Not only will you increase volumes; you may also increase the usage of the product. Do I mean to suggest that you should always enter a new market with a high price? Not at all. You should always use price to help define your market.

When creating a new market with the hope of dominating it, keep your pricing externally focused. Price early to define that market. New markets require new thinking in pricing as well as products. Pricing is never just a function of costs. Instead, it helps you define which customers you attract. That also tells you where *not* to invest resources; it becomes part of your box top. When you only invest resources in the right market, you dramatically increase your chances of sustainable success.

You can do other practical things in the market to help a business grow rapidly and sanely. I discuss some of those in Chapter 7.

Questions to Help Build a Pricing Process for New Markets

✢ Whom do you want to use the product or service?
✢ Who has a problem that *must* be solved?
✢ Is your offering a solution to a *must-solve* problem?
✢ Will the customer be able to enter new markets by using your product?
✢ If your price were higher, would it be a source of pride or pain?

✧ If your price were lower, would it be a source of pride or pain?

NOTES

1. Adapted from an article by Peter Meyer, "Creating and Dominating Markets: The CEO's Role," in *Business & Economic Review*, April 1999, pp. 9–12.
2. Personal conversation with the author (1999).
3. For some tools to use existing markets to fund new ones, please see Peter Meyer, "The Opportunity Database: Funding New Markets from Existing Businesses," in *Business Horizons*, November 1999, pp. 37–40.
4. This is a real example with fictitious names.
5. For more details on Proscar and Propecia, see Nancy Ann Jeffrey's article "Drug Shuffle for Balding Men," *Wall Street Journal*, April 13, 1999, p. B1, Western edition.
6. Paul Howes, a vice president of sales and marketing for Merck, ibid.

CHAPTER SEVEN

Applications: Build and Lead New Markets

When you decide to create new markets, you have the freedom to ask questions that you might never consider for an existing market. For instance:

- Is a less elegant product more likely to succeed?
- Can you raise your price when a client asks for a discount?
- Can you afford to fire customers?
- Can you afford to ignore your competition when it arrives?

This chapter shows some methods to apply the strategies that I have discussed so far. Again, these are not the only methods you can use; you will see that I have focused on some of the most interesting and counterintuitive ideas. Your business can apply some of these to existing markets as well.

Existing markets are easier to get into than new ones: all the pioneering work has been done by others. But entrance does not mean growth. The same resource constraints apply. Your business will never have enough time, people, or money to grow rapidly and sustainably without careful decisions. Some of those decisions are not as obvious as they might seem on the surface. Sometimes the right answer could be to raise prices when asked for a discount or to fire customers. Contrary to the common wisdom, it is often appropriate to forget about meeting your competition head-to-head. When you are stretching your resources, the counterintuitive decision may be the best one. The right place to start is with your customers.

THE ROLE OF CUSTOMERS IN EXISTING MARKETS

Markets are not products. Often, the best growth comes without great technology. Consider the work of two high-growth compa-

Chart 7-1. Platform chart for sustainable warp-speed growth.

		Pricing	Tailoring	Prospective rewards	Indies	Prospective appraisals	Killer apps	Pain
Chapter 12	Warp-Speed Growth: Managing a Business Built for Speed							
Chapters 7, 9, 11	APPLICATIONS ☞							
Chapters 6, 8, 10	INVESTMENT STRATEGY ☞	Strategy—new markets		Strategy—recruiting and structure			Strategy—effect before technology (change is bad)	
Chapters 1–5	WHAT TO INVEST ☞	Time		People			Money	
	WHERE TO INVEST ☞	Create, dominate new markets		Technology			People	
	FOUNDATION ☞	Jigsaw management—Building a box top Deciding and communicating what to work on and what to let go						

nies. America Online and the Palm Computing team produced products that the technical cognoscenti ridiculed. Both were less powerful and sophisticated than the competitors they faced, such as CompuServe, the Newton, and Windows CE handhelds. Both have dramatically outsold the other products.

The lesson is not that dumbed-down products are better. The key point to remember is that simple and easy-to-use interfaces will outsell creeping elegance every time. When you invest your resources in sophistication, you don't have them for ease of use. You are making a choice, as the developers of the Newton did. It was a great device, but the Palm brand is the one that is growing. With limited time, people, and money, you have a choice between investing in features you would like the market to have versus investing in features people will use every day. A key part of the box top of successful, sustained-growth companies is that they focus on the customer's experience. One key to success is requiring that each product be customizable by the customer.

This different emphasis (market over product) means that customers will play a different role in your growth. That role starts with letting customers define the experience that they get from your product. In this model, you don't generate a great product and let customers come. You generate a good product and *let them adapt it*. If you look at some of the most impressive growth examples from recent decades, you will see products that allow customers to tailor each use. Amazon.com offers tools to make it easy to tailor the product. America Online has "My AOL" as a central feature, giving users comprehensive control over what they get when they go on the Internet. Windows 3.0 offered the ability to let corporate users define the desktop to meet their own needs. The Palm products offer literally thousands of software and hardware variations that make the product customizable to each corporation that buys them in bulk. The Polaroid camera was the ultimate in user-defined experience. If you didn't like the picture and pose, you could get a different one immediately. IBM built the world's largest computer company on the principle that corporations could define each installation to meet their own needs.[1]

In each of these examples, the customer is someone more than a person or business with a checkbook. The customer be-

Table 7-1. Products that grew through customer involvement.

Product	Involvement Strategy
America Online	Promote tailoring of ISP to individual users with My AOL, parental controls, favorites menus, communities.
IBM 360/370 family	Promote computer programmers' ability to modify the computer to run custom applications.
Polaroid camera	Promote users' ability to design own picture and revise it as often as wanted, and still get instant results.
PalmPilot family	Design the software to make it easy for users and third parties to create thousands of applications, making each Palm product unique to the user.
Windows 3.0	Promote users' ability to create own desktop image. Custom wallpaper and icon placement seem trivial but made a considerable difference.

comes a *partner* in the use of the product and perhaps the sale. This creates a unique relationship, different from the traditional product-marketing perspective. You don't go survey what the customer wants. Instead, you go watch what the customer does with your product. Then, you design the next product to help the customer tailor the product further.

Something else happens when your business focuses on the customer experience: You divert the customer from price to effect and have the opportunity to improve your margins. Companies that have recognized this have used it to fund growth. Ultimately, they use it to help make their products and services price-independent.

RAISING YOUR PRICE WHEN ASKED FOR A DISCOUNT

Does your business discount more than you would like? When you open new markets or want to grow revenues rapidly, it is very tempting to "buy" business from customers. Discounting is easy and common. But is it better for you and for the customer?

Figure 7-1. Raising the price when asked for a discount.

1. Vendor's initial offer	$204,000
2. Customer's counter offer	$187,000
3. Vendor's second offer	$230,000
4. Customer's final response	$230,000
Final purchase price—13 percent *higher* than initial offer	

Consider this example from the early days at ROLM Corporation, a company that grew rapidly before IBM acquired it.[2] Pat started in a new territory selling computerized telephone switches (called CBXs) at an average price of $150,000. CBXs normally have a three- to six-month sales cycle, so it was a surprise when Pat got a prospect who literally wrote out and handed over a check for $187,000. It was more of a surprise when Pat refused the check.

The prospect was William, who ran his high-volume electronics company in an intensely personal way. He is the kind of committed owner who spends several nights a week on the couch in his office. William sells at a discount, and it did not take much research to see that ROLM's competitors were discounting computerized telephone switches. William wanted Pat's switch, but at a discount.

Short on time, the only appointment he would give Pat was at 10:00 P.M. Friday. Being blunt, William's way of offering to buy was to write a check on the spot from his personal checkbook, but for $17,000 below Pat's price.

As the manager or owner of a company, you will invest time, people, and money in determining the right sales price for your products. This should be the point where the value is highest. Often it is high enough to recover your costs and contribute to the profits. Then, the salesperson often discounts away thousands of dollars.

Does it need to be this way? No, it does not. Pat closed the sale that night for $230,000. Just as important, the customer thought he got a great deal. The difference that allowed Pat to raise the price when asked for a discount is the difference between involving and not involving the customer.

Raising the Price Through Involvement

Most marketing and sales strategies lead your sales teams to a situation in which they focus on their own needs and on your company. A marketing campaign creates product or company interest in the mind of your prospect, and the prospect gives your rep a few minutes to expand on it. The prospect expects your salesperson to talk about the product, and your rep is ready to do exactly that. Then the salesperson works toward the fastest possible close. Using objections as selling tools, the rep works through the customer's issues at that meeting. This model is effective in commodity sales. If you can sell on price, the model is fine. New markets, however, are rarely commodity markets. Instead, you can get more resources from customers by doing what Pat did to maximize margin contribution.

Pat operates by the maxim, "If we all come with two ears, two eyes, and one mouth, what do we always keep running?" Pat asked about William's business—not about how the switch would fit, but about the core business. Then Pat shut up and listened. Instead of pitching ROLM, Pat let William pitch his own business and what made it run.

Pat was looking for two things that marketing doesn't do well. Pat wanted to find both the hot buttons of the owner and the places where ROLM's software would make a difference. With that software, Pat knew ROLM could tailor the installation to match William's business needs. From experience, Pat knew that William and his people could help define the experience that they wanted from the software, making them a part of the design process. Pat also knew, after listening for about thirty seconds, that William would want a discount. Software was the key to avoiding it, and Pat planned to get a higher margin.

The best way Pat knows to do that is to understand the business, and Pat used questions designed to make sure that the owner learned as much as Pat did. Both learned a lot from that conversation. But Pat wanted to know things William didn't yet know about his own business.

The Next Steps—Survey and Design Session

Before the Friday night meeting, Pat went to six key managers and two key salespeople and asked them about the business. Pat was specifically looking for information that William might not have. There was, and will always be, plenty of this. It took four hours, but Pat left knowing the business inside out.

That Friday night, William had his defenses up, waiting to be sold, ready to ask for the discount. Pat surprised him. The conversation did not start with how wonderful the product and ROLM were. Pat started with the key levers for William's business and how William's team would want to tailor the machine to fit those levers. William found himself in a conversation about defining the experience for his own people and customers.

Stop here and consider. How would you react to this? Most of us would do what William did—get very interested in new knowledge.

During the Friday night meeting, Pat described some benefits that William's company could use. Pat did not describe the software or opportunities that would not apply to William. The focus was on how William could tailor the CBX to meet the company's exact needs. Pat was careful to describe the options that William could have and ask William to weigh the costs and benefits. Pat did not tell William; it was up to William to assign benefits. Pat knew what William's staff thought and was careful to make sure William knew as well.

Pat brought his manager, Fred, along but made Fred promise not to talk about how wonderful ROLM was as a company. Pat only presented the benefits and the cost of getting those benefits. William started to weigh those costs against the benefits.

At the end of the session, Pat totaled up the benefits and the costs. Pat then asked for the $204,000. At this point, William smiled and wrote out the check for $187,000, and Pat said no.

The Close

It was Fred's first call with Pat, and Fred had to struggle to keep quiet. He watched and thought about how he might have to fire Pat on Monday morning. Fred was wondering where he would find another salesperson for the territory and how he could still get William's check for $187,000. Then Pat said that William could have an even better deal. By moving up to the next-model CBX, William's business could have access to software that would allow William to tailor his experience even more. This was a function Pat knew William would want his business to have.

Pat suggested that the list price on that configuration would be $280,000. Pat offered to take a check for that machine at a price of $230,000 and try to get it approved over the weekend.

That was a bluff. Fred was doing the math in his head. Most of the additional price was high-margin software. In fact, the discounted $230,000 deal had more margin than the original $204,000 package at full price! It was a great deal for the company. Fred knew he could approve it. Better yet, he might not have to fire Pat.

William did his own math. He wanted the software's benefits and knew it would help his business perform tasks worth well more than the $43,000 difference between his initial offer and Pat's second proposal. William knew it was a good deal for his company, as did Pat. The close was a simple question: "Is this a good deal for your business?"

Pat and Fred walked out with a check for a high-margin deal. William asked for a discount, paid an increased price, and became one of Pat's best references.

This process has been done often. It brings benefit to both the customer and the vendor. As you enter new markets, make it a principle of your business always to build involvement into products and to sell the benefits of that involvement. Avoid commodity behavior. Your box top can focus your team away from that.

USING A 7-STEP SALES PROCESS TO GET HIGHER MARGINS

In the deal with William and in other projects, Pat followed a basic sales process that enables a salesperson to raise the margins. The process is much more resource-intensive than other processes. For a commodity or low-cost product, this sales process requires too much time for each deal. However, if you are selling an intangible or high-value product that uses direct sales, this process can deliver you better results than the traditional qualify, present, and close techniques.

The key to Pat's success is a 7-Step Process that involves the customer in the decision and promotes tailoring of the solution. In some research across several lines of business, I found that three things occur when companies use the process: (1) The 7-step process takes twice as many hours as the traditional process. (2) Because the business needs of the customer drive the deal, sales close sooner. Customers don't wait for the end of a quarter to get the biggest discount; they order quickly to get the product sooner. (3) If the salesperson gets through the fourth step, the deal closes at full margin more than 90 percent of the time. The investment of time can clearly be seen to pay off.

The process runs like this:

Step 1. Make cold calls, whether from referrals or from a list. Pat is careful to choose whom to talk to on the first call. Not all leads from the same prospective customer are of equal value. You will be better off making an effort to be sure that you start at the correct place in the prospect's organization.

Step 2. Make the introductory call. Most salespeople spend this call talking about their company. However, Pat gives only a brief description of what the company has done for others and quickly moves along to the problem that the prospect needs resolved. Pat's company gets almost no attention.

The problem the prospect needs resolved is the only subject that really matters. His or her most important problem is paramount, even if it does not directly involve the sales rep's product. Pat works to identify that problem. If the conversation heads toward the product, Pat will try to make sure that the prospect has first discussed the business issues that keep him or her awake at night. Then Pat works to get an agreed-upon definition of success for solving that problem.

Step 3. Survey the stakeholders. Few prospective clients have a single decision maker. Most have several decision makers, who usually disagree on the success criteria for the key issues. Often, they don't even agree on which issues are key.

Pat, as an outsider, talks to the key stakeholders to get a view of the problem from several sides. Each stakeholder supplies his or her definition of success. This survey is a key step. It can take four to eight hours, but getting the whole picture leads to identifying the whole solution.

Step 4. Hold a design session. Pat wants buy-in from the stakeholders so that the work actually results in a solution, not just a sale. In this session, Pat shows these key people what came out of the survey and how the results might define the problem. These become the success criteria for the project. It is important to consider all costs for the work, not just Pat's. No project is accomplished without a cost of additional time, people, money, and opportunity. It is a disservice to the customer to take that into account for your own business but not for the prospect's. With William, Pat did not invite other stakeholders to the session but did make sure that William knew what they wanted and what other costs they had identified.[3]

Pat and the customer focus on solutions, not on costs and fees. The focus on the results of the work is the key to avoiding last-minute discounts. The more important the overall solution is, the less attention Pat's cost gets.

At the end of the design session, the stakeholders have defined the severity of the issue, the need for a solution, the criteria for measuring success, and a plan to solve it. The costs are a small part of the discussion. They are insignificant compared with the value of resolving the problem.

Step 5. Document the meeting. This documentation becomes the proposal. Pat alters the proposal to be short and focus on the benefits. A single page may be enough. Investing resources in elegant proposals here does not generate a return for Pat's company.

Step 6. Get a contract both parties like. If Pat has done a good job of identifying the most important problem and showing a path to resolution, the customer executives want to bypass the contract step. For important issues, who wants to slow for paperwork?

Step 7. Do the work and follow up. Pat asks what the next most critical issues are and proposes solutions where appropriate. In effect, Pat starts the process again. With all the knowledge and contacts, the second and third sales are much less time-intensive than the first.

7-Step Sales Process

1. Prospecting, finding the right contact.
2. Initial call, talking less about the product and more about the customer.
3. Survey, asking for input from the stakeholders.
4. Design session, asking for agreement on solving the important problem.
5. Proposal, documenting the design session.
6. Close, usually a formality.
7. Follow up, asking for the next most important issue to resolve.

USING MARKETING TO CONSERVE RESOURCES

The 7-step process worked because Pat used an involvement approach to sell the business benefits, not the product features. You can use marketing to help your sales teams do the same. Both the process and the marketing steps are simple.

Marketing provides two functions that are useful to a rapidly growing company and one that is not. The useful functions are creating an image of value to the reader or viewer and causing specific action. The function that is not useful is building your company's own self-image. Nonetheless, that is where most marketing resources get invested.

As an example, take this morning's copy of the *Wall Street Journal* (or any magazine or paper that would advertise to your key audience) and look at the ads. If you don't have a copy handy, use the following two lists.[4] Flip through the publication and look at the full-page ads. You will see two kinds of advertisements. The first group represents most display ads; the second group represents the minority. Look at the headlines, the attention-getting text, from each ad.

Group 1: *Headlines Reflecting the Predominant Style of Display Ads in the* Wall Street Journal

- ✩ Saab vs. the Filibuster[5]
- ✩ Fresh Air to Fresh Food, Nuclear Makes It Happen[6]
- ✩ Of All the Things Grand Cherokee Can Escape From, Distinction Isn't One of Them[7]
- ✩ All for one[8]
- ✩ 1 company[9]
- ✩ Combining outstanding relationships and capabilities, Chase is now number two in high grade debt.[10]

Group 2: *Headlines Reflecting the Minority Style of Display Ads in the* Wall Street Journal

- ✩ Schwab is looking for 1000 people who want to change the way the world invests.[11]
- ✩ You sweated blood to build your own company. That's probably why you're the wrong person to put a value on it.[12]
- ✩ Companies that know the Internet best use Oracle for e-business. Do you?[13]
- ✩ What do you feed a growing business?[14]
- ✩ How to have a tax-free retirement.[15]

The key difference between the two sets of ads is the focus. The ads in the first group focus directly on the advertiser. The headlines do not try to involve the reader or suggest any benefit to the reader. They promote the company.

The ads in the second group attempt to involve the reader or offer a direct benefit to the reader. Lay your ads out on a table and ask which ones are most attractive. When we do this with executives in workshops, they routinely answer that the minority ads—the ones that focus on involvement of and benefit to the reader—are more attractive.

A friend calls this the "Enough about you, let's talk about me" syndrome. Most marketing suffers from it. This behavior does no real harm to your relationship with your customers if they ignore it. It may, if imaginative, get you considerable attention. One Silicon Valley software company ran ads of the company president in a stunning black dress. She looked attractive, and the ads got a lot of buzz. They did not build the business.

It costs you a fair amount of resources to create, edit, approve, and distribute any kind of marketing materials. The worst thing about self-promotional marketing materials is that all such ads or brochures or sales pitches carry an opportunity cost. Marketing that makes a call to action or stresses a benefit usually costs no more than self-focused work, and it usually results in a better boost for your growth. When you are trying to sustain rapid growth, examine your marketing and try to exclude self-promotion from the box top. Instead, use your resources to tell the customer what he or she gets.

Developing Involvement into Products

One of the side effects of the miniaturization of processors is that you can put a processor in almost any product that sells for more than twenty-five American cents. For many companies, this has become a near-fatal opportunity. The temptation to creeping elegance, discussed in Chapter 10, results in features and capabilities that consume resources but don't attract buyers. Worse, they distract the manufacturers. The company invests resources in the wrong areas.

However, in low-priced products that you sell through wide distribution, the opportunity to boost growth with on-board processing is real. If your product can use this processing power to enable users to adapt it, it will have the opportunity to create its own markets and applications. Network end devices (such as remote hubs) that are self-configuring and adapt to the changing needs of the local users would save countless hours of corporate staff time. Dozens of VCRs are on the market, but none (yet) use processing to learn the user's habits and adapt to them. Electronic pill bottles are a research item at this writing, but the potential is there to offer a product that will learn a patient's needs and help him or her remember to take medicine. Given how inventive people are, you can be fairly sure that some will find applications that you did not consider. If people use

Palm handhelds to unlock their cars, they will find some use you did not consider for a VCR.

Look at what you make and then consider the very low cost of processing power. Ask whether you could use that power to make your product adaptive.

Firing Customers

It turns out that some customers do not repay your resource investment as well as others. When that is the case, you run the risk of expending more resources to get less growth. In other words, chasing the customers who fall outside your box top may cost you opportunities elsewhere.

For your box top, there will always be a core group of customers who buy into the idea and will pay for the effect. Then there will always be a more peripheral group of customers that sort of buy the idea but are not an easy sell. By extending the line, discounting the products, and exerting considerable management and sales effort, you can get most of that peripheral group to buy. It may cost you far more resources than it is worth.

As you think about new prospects and reselling to old ones, consider that many of them will not be worth the effort. They will feel free to fire you if you do not perform. Why should you not feel free to do the same to them for not helping you meet your box top?

Some companies fire their bottom tier of employees every year. Consider doing the same with your least profitable customers. Not every customer is worth the resources you expend to keep them.

Ignore the Competition?

One of the most popular reasons to have more customers is to stop others from having them. It is a great way to keep the sales team motivated, but is it a good strategy for growing your business?

If you are creating a new market, the issue is time to acceptance. There, the controlling factors are not the competition as much as your ability to read and take advantage of the opportunity. Doing as well as Crixivan—not the first product to market but the product that became the standard for treatment—wouldn't be so bad. Instead of focusing on the competition, use your resources to focus on what it will take to be adaptive and attractive.

If you are in an existing market, you can change to meet the competition in that market. However, as you do, remember that the market is changing as well. What was acceptable for VCRs last year will not work now, no matter what the competitors do. Financial products that do the competition one better will not necessarily be attractive for your customers.

Given your limited resources, you have a choice: You can study either your competitor or your market. If you choose to do the latter, you will be one step ahead, planning products that users can adapt to their own needs and that are inherently more attractive.

Ask yourself, In a new market, what do my competitors know that I do not? The answer should be "Nothing." Don't waste resources that your business could use to make your product and company better than the competition's.

Notes

1. This happened well before the IBM PC was introduced. The value of the 360/370 architecture was that it allowed corporate buyers to create new applications and uses for enormous, expensive computers. That philosophy eventually became the dominant characteristic of the open PC software platform.
2. The story is true, but the names of the individuals have been changed.
3. Pat and William's design session is not fully described here. If you would like to see a more detailed description, please drop the author a note at Peter@MeyerGrp.com. We'll send you a much more detailed version.
4. The advertisements mentioned here are all from the *Wall*

Street Journal's Western edition, April 13, 1999. They are typical of the ads that appear most days in the paper.
5. © 1999 SAAB CARS USA.
6. © 1999 Nuclear Energy Institute.
7. © 1999 Daimler Chrysler.
8. © 1999 Teligent, Inc.
9. © 1999 Delphi Automotive Systems.
10. © 1999 The Chase Manhattan Corporation.
11. © 1999 Charles Schwab & Co., Inc.
12. © 1999 KPMG LLP.
13. © 1999 Oracle Corporation. All rights reserved. Oracle is a trademark of Oracle Corporation.
14. © 1999 Compaq Computer Corporation. All rights reserved.
15. © 1999 Dean Witter Reynolds, Inc.

CHAPTER EIGHT

Resource Strategies: Growth, People, and Structure

Rapid growth inextricably intertwines people and time. The people on whom you rely can gain you time to do the work that enables growth and new markets. Or they can suck time and energy away from you and cripple the business's ability to expand. A company that is growing slowly has room for both the day-to-day work and the time to invest in future management of performers. In rapid growth, your business can't afford the time. When people can't deliver the results you plan, rapid growth is compromised. (See Figure 8-1 on page 124.)

Every manager has the responsibility to manage people well one on one. The owner or general manager also has to ensure that he or she organizes the business to get and keep the very best people. In this chapter and the next, we'll look at some strategies and applications to use that second resource in the best possible way. These are ideas and tools that may work well for you or may get in the way of your business. As you consider each, as well as other tools I can't cover here, compare them against your box top for the business. If they appeal to you but do not fit the business, they are not right. As important as people and good strategies are, they are not more important than the overall strategy of the business.

When your organization starts to grow rapidly, the role of general manager or owner changes. For stable organizations, that role is primarily leadership. Rapid growth requires an equal blend of excellent leadership and attention to the right structure.

Chart 8-1. Platform chart for sustainable warp-speed growth.

Chapter 12	Warp-Speed Growth: Managing a Business Built for Speed							
Chapters 7, 9, 11	APPLICA-TIONS ☞	Pricing	Tailoring	Prospective rewards	Indies	Prospective appraisals	Killer apps	Pain
Chapters 6, 8, 10	INVEST-MENT STRATEGY ☞	Strategy—new markets		Strategy—recruiting and structure			Strategy—effect before technology (change is bad)	
Chapters 1–5	WHAT TO INVEST ☞	Time		People			Money	
	WHERE TO INVEST ☞	Create, dominate new markets		Technology			People	
	FOUNDA-TION ☞	Jigsaw management—Building a box top Deciding and communicating what to work on and what to let go						

The senior executive becomes responsible for ensuring that the business recruits the right people and is organized to let them do great work.

This chapter focuses on companywide issues that will help you get and keep the best people. We'll look at whom to recruit and how to structure to help them produce the best results. Chapter 9 discusses strategies to use that structure in one-on-one management.

Most owners and managers work to attract people who are self-starters, capable of delivering specific results without requiring much time and attention. You recruit carefully, but not every person with whom you work will have these attributes. In a gradual-growth organization, you'll have time to help someone grow into a job. In rapid growth, that time costs you opportunities elsewhere.

It never ceases to amaze me that people who work so well in one place fail in another. Is it their fault or ours? One of the most important messages from the teachings of W. Edwards Deming is that people are almost never the problem: They are the victims of a bad process or choice.[1] Assigning blame is not important; fixing the problem is. The general manager or owner is the person who can fix systemic issues or demand that they be

Figure 8-1. Need for focus on structure.

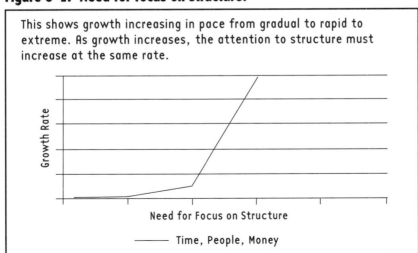

This shows growth increasing in pace from gradual to rapid to extreme. As growth increases, the attention to structure must increase at the same rate.

Growth Rate

Need for Focus on Structure

——— Time, People, Money

fixed. In that role, the senior executive has the control to establish a good process. You can make it possible for good people to succeed and to give you time to work on creating and dominating new markets.

Three manifestations will grow as the business does, and they will remain inseparable:

1. The business will grow as you feed it resources.

2. In a rapid-growth business, you will not be able to recruit as many good people as you need, even with the strategies discussed in this chapter.

3. In order to keep up, you will have to depend on the growth of your people. People are the only resource that you can hope to stretch a little as the workload increases. Structuring for the growth of people is a key to sane and stable business growth.

As your people grow, you must do the same. What you did last year will not be correct next year, and no one can help you make that transition as well as you can. A good place to start is with the way your business handles recruiting and structure.

RECRUITING AND STRUCTURING FOR GROWTH

In a stable organization, you have room and time to move people around to the right job. In rapid growth, you need to be prepared to live with the people you choose. During rapid and extreme growth, structuring for recruiting and performance is more important—and more difficult. Because it all starts there, you may want to change your recruiting model.

One of the most important and difficult changes in the workforce over the past two decades has been the rise and independence of experts. Almost every industry now has a core of people who are expert in skills that change too rapidly for non-experts to keep up. Two decades ago, anyone could tune the engine in his or her car. Now, the amount of electronics makes it difficult to do that without specific training and equipment. Thirty years ago, managing personnel rules and issues was an add-on task many companies gave to administrative staffs. Today, the changing regulations and the difficulty of recruiting have made it nearly impossible to avoid problems without a trained specialist. People who specialized in refinancing mortgages were scarce twenty years ago. Now, they are common. In a few years, they may be gone again. Only a few years ago, the changes in software were obvious enough that a manager could keep up. Now, it is nearly impossible for a manager to both run the business and evaluate what software designers are doing.

Most of these effects are well documented in works about knowledge workers. One of the less obvious results is the change in where you go to find your talent.

RECRUITING TALENT WITHOUT HIRING

The good news about the economy is that unemployment is down—and there's more money available for people to spend on your products. The bad news is that everyone has a job and fewer of the right people are available to work for you. In your product market, you compete with only a few key players. In recruiting, you may compete with hundreds. This problem is one of the two that consistently keep CEOs up at night.[2]

To bring the right resources to key opportunities, you can initiate a different model. It does not replace traditional recruiting practices but accompanies them. Following this model, which is outlined in the balance of the chapter, will cause some changes throughout your organization. It will require leadership effort to change how your managers look at recruiting. That takes the issue out of the realm of human resources (HR) and makes it the responsibility of line management.[3]

Competition for the Best People

The competition for recruiting gets great press in the technology arena, but the problem is much more widespread. Even in the industrial Midwest, Kay Casey, of Standard Register, notes, "We run ads now and get one or two responses. We used to get thirty or forty before."[4]

Much of what your company does today may make the problem worse. Providing co-op programs, holding job fairs, recruiting out of schools and halfway houses, increasing benefits, and offering signing bonuses are all necessary and good. But they deliver diminishing results. Raiding your best competitors provides a solution—but it's only a matter of time until they, in turn, raid you right back. Instead of providing you with a solution, these tactics increase the competition as others engage in the same practices.

Your business needs other ways to get the brightest and best minds focused on your most important problems.

Minds, Not People

Start by asking what you need. For some positions, you need lots of good people to perform an ongoing role. For those, you can get away with hiring in bulk. You count on losing some of these employees as part of the process, and that is acceptable. But sometimes, churning people will not work. You need single, specific skills and backgrounds. For these, you want the best minds.

Why minds and not people? Superb strategy execution is a result of individual efforts combined into a whole. When you put a person on a key task that requires judgment and experience, you are betting your strategy on that individual choice. An average mind will produce results far inferior to the best.

The distinction between minds and bodies is control. Many managers are used to controlling people, but they know they cannot control minds. With a great mind, you aim it in the right direction and keep it excited. As venture capitalist Ann Winblad notes, "A capital-efficient, people-driven company is not an assembly line; it is a community of skilled craftsmen able to make decisions at every level."[5] You can throw bodies at some tasks, but for execution of key strategies, the issue is which individual minds you apply.

Where would you apply a best mind? Many of your development projects require that kind of intellect. Writing code that delivers results but does not increase your support costs requires a better-than-average mind. Some key customer relationships deserve the best minds you can get. Solving production problems so they stay solved requires a superior mind. Positioning products to get high margins needs more than the average thought process. You may have ten or twenty important projects that never seem to get completed. Would an exceptional mind with the right background help you bring these to completion?

It is tempting to compromise. The fact is that the best minds are hard to find and harder to get on your side. It is much easier to put a "warm body" into a spot and then wait for a better person to come along. The compromise person may not be great at the job and may need more attention than the right person, but some work gets done meanwhile. You can't blame the person; he or she was put into a no-win situation.

The cost of doing that is not simply the cost of the salary. You are paying the cost of the time you and others have to invest to compensate for a poor situation. You cannot recover this time later; it's gone forever. You have spent opportunity.

The bad news is that some of the best minds in the business are not available to you as employees. They have decided to opt out of the corporate environment. These minds will never respond to a recruiting pitch for a job. They would not be likely to stay even if you got them to accept that pitch. They are not money- and benefits-driven. They are project- and idea-driven.

What are these people? I call them "Indies," for independent minds. The name intentionally evokes the image of Indiana Jones, the brilliant, highly independent, very successful archaeologist hero of the movie trilogy. If these are the Indies, you are the museum or government that contracts for results. Your goal is to have someone go get the Ark of the Covenant.

For many jobs, you would hire full-time employees. For finding the Ark, you would want someone with the skills of an Indiana Jones. You know, almost without having to think about it, that you can't and won't make Jones an employee. But to have him acting on your behalf in a self-motivated way will be very valuable to you and your search. So you ask him to achieve a clear objective, one that attracts him. He goes after it with skills you could not hire. He is an Indy.

In your real world, many projects need the brains and self-motivation of an Indy. The good news is that if you can't hire them, neither can anyone else. But maybe you can attract their minds to your needs.

Example Indies

To give you a sense of their motivation and mind-set, let me introduce you to several typical Indies.[6]

Joan. Joan is one of the best root-cause analysis and process minds in the country. If you have a nasty, customer-affecting problem that keeps recurring, Joan is exactly the sort of person whom you want to solve it. Getting to the root of this sort of problem excites her. Teaching your people to do the same is part of what she enjoys. She works fast and well and does very high-quality work.

Joan has worked for a university and a large computer company. She will never work for a corporation again. In fact, she won't work for a boss again. She doesn't need to, and she doesn't want to.

Oscar. Oscar writes communications software for fun. These are work products that he can produce in months and a company can then sell for millions of dollars. And by introducing new capabilities, they move the market forward. Oscar can help a business create and dominate new markets.

Oscar has worked for large software firms and a hardware company. He will never work for a boss again. He writes good

Figure 8-2. Differentiating people and minds.

People	Minds
—Can be recruited and hired in quantity	—Must be recruited and hired individually
—Are hard to find	—Are very hard to find
—Are part of normal labor pool	—Have often opted out of corporate life
—Look for average	—Look for special
—Expect turnover	—Structure to avoid turnover
—Accept control philosophy	—Reject control philosophy
—Can be used for operational tasks	—Should be saved for strategic tasks
—May become excited about work	—Are always excited about work
—Are often traditional employees, contractors	—Are Indies

software because *he* enjoys it. Oscar does not collect a paycheck. Often, he receives no money at all, instead taking his payment in stock.

Pat. Pat listens well. By asking good questions, he can identify the core business problem and show people how to solve it. He helps companies smooth incoming revenue so that it doesn't all appear at the end of the quarter. He helps companies to find revenue where they are missing it and to increase margins.

Pat does not work for a boss. His attitude is, "Been there, done that, got the T-shirts." He helped someone find $2 billion in otherwise unidentified prospects but won't take a salary. Pat likes to know that he can fire companies whenever they get boring.

Joan, Oscar, and Pat are typical Indies. There are thousands of people like them—expert minds you'd love to have in your business. You can't hire them, but you can rent them for a few dollars and a very interesting problem. When you start to define your needs as minds, not employees, you start to open yourself up to this pool. These are the people you can get and the people you want working on your most pressing problems and opportunities.

Indies flow into and ebb out of your business under two symbiotic conditions: One is that you need them; the other is that they are interested in working on your problem. They are not telecommuters; they are the true virtual workforce—minds that are there when you need them and gone when you do not.

Using minds in this way is so counterintuitive that few companies will do it. That gives you an advantage in recruiting. Having fewer companies competing for the best talent pool substantially increases your chances of getting the great mind you need.

But this is all contrary to how we run businesses today. Using Indies probably violates your internal rules and practices. Your legal and HR teams can show you fifty reasons not to do it. Your line managers will need guidelines so they can start to change how they do recruiting. This structural change will require the leadership of the owner or general manager.

Finding and Using Indies

To get the best minds doing your most important work may require a change in the structure of the work in your organization. (See Table 8-1 on page 135.) Try the following strategies:

✢ Start by making your most important work as interesting as possible. Indies work for themselves and for fun as much as for money. To attract them, build up opportunities for self-actualization as much as you do for money or health plans. Winblad notes, "We can attract talent by offering two kinds of opportunities; to contribute to a vision for the future, and to share in the rewards."[7] Structure for both.

✢ Know and then target whom you want. Instead of using HR to go to brokers to get more candidates and contractors, get your *line* people to look in places where individual Indies hang out. Your line managers are the ones who can define the opportunity best. They are the ones who can recognize the right talents.

✢ Depending on the skill set, each Indy has a network he or she likes to work with and talk to. It might be a Usenet group on the Internet; it might be a particular conference. A good place to start is to ask several of your knowledgeable people to participate in Usenet groups. Have them pick the lists that focus on the kind of work with which you want the most help. This will require a great deal of patience, but if one or two key people come from that, it will be worth it.

✢ When you begin to find Indies, be sure you do not take people who are good. Only take the "insanely great." Check references and don't cut corners because they are not permanent hires.

✢ Set up the right flexibility. Be sure you have an HR person who is proficient at contracting with individuals and willing to treat Indies as businesspeople, not employees. Be prepared to make innovative deals that reward for results, even if it means paying for performance.

✢ Reduce the "pain" of working for you. Don't ask Indies to go to staff meetings or serve on task forces. Don't require them to work in your office. If your company is slow to pay, be sure you pay these people on time. They help you best when they are focused on your work, not on your administrative process.

✧ Make your own Indies if you have to. You may find people who are employed elsewhere today but thinking of leaving tomorrow. Stan, a vice president at a high-tech company, is one of the best operations troubleshooters in the country. He will leave his present company this year, but not for another company. He will follow his dream to become independent. Stan could use the support. You can provide that. Instead of trying to hire him, consider putting Stan (and others like him) in business as a sole practitioner. Then become his first client. He will be happier, and you will have the mind you want. You can grow your markets as you help him realize his dream.

✧ Ask the work team to sit together for two hours before they start. Many Indies (and your own good people) have little patience for classic team-building exercises. However, most will respond to a request to come to the office to negotiate and set success criteria for a project. Start with introductions and a little chat, but make this a very high content meeting. Ask the team to return with an action plan that identifies specific definitions of success. You want all the participants to be focused on the results and excited about them.

✧ Corporations typically want to control their resources. However, access to these minds is more important than that control. To get the best people, you have to change your habits as an organization. To get the best results, remember that these experts are most effective if you let them work at the top of Maslow's hierarchy of needs.[8] Let them produce results from their *own* processes. And let them do it from their *own* location if it helps.

✧ Take the time to structure the work to be interesting from the start. It will excite the people you rely on and make them more likely to innovate for you.

Strategies to Attract and Keep the Best Minds

✧ Build opportunities for self-actualization.
✧ Have your best line managers recruit.

✧ Recruit where the people are, not where you want them to be.
✧ Become known for not compromising on people; only bring in the "insanely great."
✧ Reduce the "pain" of working with your organization.
✧ Put employees into business as consultants instead.
✧ Manage through success criteria.
✧ Structure the work to be interesting from the start.

Solve the Right Problem: The Structure of the Work

The first element in changing the structure of the work is to measure Indies on results. Results that they can measure are inherently more interesting than activities, and achieving results is inherently more exciting than ticking off activities. Strategies to set and measure results follow in Chapter 9, but the decision to structure work around results instead of activities starts here.

You can begin now in a small way. Somewhere in your organization, you have a person who is failing at his or her task. Ask whether this person is the first to fail there. When two or more people fail at a task, it is an indication that the problem is not the person but the work or process. Instead of putting another person in that role, change the requirements.

To do this, look at the way your business measures the work. Is the measurement capturing a specific result, or is it quantifying activities? If the latter, go to the person who is doing the work and ask him or her to define the right result. Set a box top for the right result—one that would work for this person and for the people who use the work product—but don't recommend that result. Follow the jigsaw management appraisal model in the following chapter, and try to structure the output of the work around the result.

One word of caution: Be careful not to run afoul of the rules concerning the distinction between employees and contract workers. The penalties are serious. Make sure that you find the latest interpretations of the regulations and follow them.

All over your industry, companies are trying to hire the very best and hardest-to-find minds. These are workers who are motivated by results and can and will deliver those results if given the right environment. Your company can be the one that gets the cream of this crop. They are brilliant, different, and extremely valuable. And they will never work for a larger company again. Get them on your key efforts and save your competitive recruiting efforts for other positions.

Right and Wrong Expectations

There is a lot of talk about virtual teams and alternative workforces, with many disappointments. Why the latter? Because unreasonable expectations get set. Some common but *incorrect* expectations are:

✧ The cost of people and benefits will drop. You will find that using virtual experts and Indies is not cheap. Save these people for the key projects, where the value of the result is very high. Don't invest key people in projects that aren't important.

✧ Uninteresting work will get done by contractors. Indies are people who are excited and rewarded by the task. When it gets unexciting, they may opt out. This means restructuring some work to make it interesting.

✧ Infrastructure costs will decrease. Minds and ideas, not bricks and mortar, are what make results happen for you. Sometimes that costs you less; sometimes it does not. Either way, focus on the effect, not the cost to produce it.

✧ You'll reduce the risk of bad hires. Putting the wrong mind on a task will hurt no matter whether it is a permanent hire or a short-term assignee. You can get rid of the assignee with less effort, but that does not help you to get the result you need.

So what are the correct expectations? Plan to:

✧ Break your own rules to attract and use the right minds. Some great minds are available, even if they do not meet your normal hiring standards and you don't meet their standards for a good employer. The senior executives need to endorse the idea of contracting Indies so that the team members are willing to try even though they might fail.

✧ Define clearly stated success criteria. Indies want this because they respond best to a clear definition of success, a goal on which they can focus. You want to know when they are done so that you can end the relationship or give them another assignment.

✧ Move your people who are doing the wrong jobs to the right assignments. Why is your vice president of engineering trying to design interfaces? An Indy could do that faster and free up the VP to do tasks only he or she could perform. Successful growth depends on using both resources correctly.

✧ Focus on results instead of control. Indies have climbed Maslow's pyramid; they like self-actualization. They work best when they work for that internal sense of contribution. Traditional bosses need control as a tool, but Indies feel that it's claustrophobic and that it diminishes their sense of contribution. Indies left the control-oriented corporate environment long ago. They will often refuse to work in another one. They don't have to.[9]

Table 8-1. What drives Indies to work for you and to wander away from you.

To Work for You	To Wander Away from You
Work *they* find challenging	Boring tasks
Results orientation	Activity management
A chance to use their minds	Excess meetings, administrivia
Independence	Bosses
A sense of real contribution	
Clear goals	

STRUCTURE FOR GROWTH—ORCHESTRAS

You can look in dozens of books for tips on organizational structure, but no single structure will be right for your business. Instead, you will need to consider the correct blend. More important, the structure that works well on the pages of a great book will not necessarily work well with your people, customers, and products. Instead of reviewing a dozen different alternatives from others, consider starting with a simple concept and tailoring it to fit your growth.

A good starting place is the orchestra model suggested by Peter Drucker.[10] My idea behind suggesting it is simple: You are not as smart as you'd like to think. As good as you are at the tasks you did last year, it is becoming impossible to know the work and manage the organization simultaneously. Your experience and information are dated and are becoming more so by the hour. You are getting dumber.

With limited resources in periods of rapid growth, each manager has to make a decision—try to do the job of management or try keep up with the technologies and skills. You do not have enough time to do both.

Orchestras are designed to handle this. Each member of an orchestra has skill in a limited area but in great depth. A percussionist is just as important as an oboist, but the percussionist could not replace the oboist. A second violinist can listen to both and understand what they are doing but can't perform the work of either.

The first violinist has a unique role—that of example. You would not ask the first violinist to choose the music for concerts or decide how to interpret it. You ask him or her to focus on producing the best results possible from the instrument. The violinist does the work. The conductor provides the definition of best possible results.

The conductor is also a specialist. He or she can do none of the work of the other specialists. You would never ask the conductor to replace one of the violinists in a pinch. The conductor has two different responsibilities. The first is to help the players produce the best possible music as individuals. The second is to help them produce the best possible results as a group. These skills are different from those of any of the players. This work takes all of the conductor's time and experience. Often, the conductor will start in the same way as the general manager or owner of a rapidly growing business. The conductor will set up a box top—defining success for the players. Each player knows how the music should sound. A good conductor will not tell the experts how to achieve that success, but he or she will find a way to make that achievement occur.

The result: an organization optimized for performance. An orchestra's management chain is as short as possible; the results are as good as you can get. With little waste on overhead, the players produce music instead of reports and staff meetings.

As you grow your business, ask yourself how you would handle your team as an orchestra. You won't create one, but the thought process might cause you to change how you structure your organization. You will have groups of specialists who, like the percussionist, do work that your managers (conductors) can't fully understand. The managers have the option of either telling the player how to do the job or telling the player what results to produce.

If you were to structure your customer service organization as a community builds an orchestra, you might invest the time and money in more skilled service representatives who are more skilled. Perhaps you would recruit Indies, knowing that you could treat them as such. You would ask managers to set objectives based on results, not process, and to focus on their own results, not the process to get those results (see Chapter 9). Each shift would have a lead service rep (first violinist), but you would not ask that rep to be responsible for the performance of the others—only for setting an example. This might sound familiar; many customer support organizations are structured the same way.

This has implications beyond recruiting. It will cause you to change some existing teams. For instance, if you structure your finance department with more expert specialists, what would happen to managers who can't delegate well? Many of the less skilled specialists would grow quickly when working with the new experts. What about the people who don't? You will need to have a plan to work with both.

If your development group is to match the orchestral model, will you have to find a manager who is a conductor, not a doer? Do you need someone to tell the development team what box top (results) you require and then help them to produce those results individually and as a group? You might find that contemplating an orchestral model will cause you to hire different managers and to handle promotions entirely differently. The key to making it work is not just the number of people and managers; it is what you ask the people and managers to do. I discuss these topics in the next chapter.

EFFECTS VS. PROCESS—THE NATURE OF THE WORK

If you use the orchestral model, or any other, the nature of the jobs might have to change. In order to make this work in your customer service organization, you will need to:

- ✧ Allow the service representatives to focus on the quality of the work they are doing
- ✧ Define their own tasks to be more interesting to them

Just as Hawkins and Sachtlaben in the examples in Chapter 10, you will need to ask the people on whom you rely to do something different. They will need to emphasize the effect over the process.

This partly depends on practicality: There will be no one around to evaluate the processes they use. It partly depends on attracting and keeping the best minds. They will know more about processes than their managers. If that is not true at the start, it will be soon afterward.

As an example, let's return to jigsaw puzzles. When you assemble a puzzle, you have several strategies from which to choose. You can sort by shape, by color, or by drawings and lines on the pieces. You could decide to start with the edges, if you can find them. If others are helping, you could choose to assign roles or let people just play.

In a series of approximately fifty tests, we asked teams of managers and executives to assemble custom-made jigsaw puzzles in a short time.[11] The instructions are brief: "Assemble this today." All the teams assembled the puzzles correctly and in the time given. Most had fun doing it.

We called Stave Puzzles, the manufacturer, and asked the

experts there to tell us the quickest way to get the puzzles assembled. After each team was done, we offered to explain the secret. After hearing it, most of the managers and executives told us it was wrong.

Who is right here? The expert (Stave) or the team doing the work? The work was done to specification, with little time invested by the manager (us). What if we had invested more time?

We tried that. Of the 150 teams, we told the secret to around 30. We tried to get many of them to follow the "officially sanctioned" path first. Those 30 teams also assembled the puzzles. However, they were slower on average. The ones we pushed were the slowest of all. They also had the least fun. It seems that the more time we invest in how, the worse off we all are. When we defined success and let the teams follow a supposedly suboptimal process, we got the best results.

As the owner or general manager, you get to set a tone of focusing on effect. People may get the right results by doing the wrong things. Your choice: Make sure that they know how to define the right results. Set the box top and don't invest either your time or theirs in trying to tell them how to assemble the puzzle.

THE EFFECTS OF CHANGING STRUCTURES

Changing structure could change your organization's compensation plan. You would pay for results instead of the process to achieve them, and this would apply to employees and Indies. You and almost everyone else in the organization will need to establish success criteria for each key result. You'll need box tops for everything you want to measure. This represents a substantial investment of time. You might need to change your recruiting strategy and look more for people who resemble Indies. All these changes will feel like heresy to many people. You will need to endorse the concept continually so that people don't fall back into old habits under pressure. You will have to invest time and people in all this.

Could you bring five or fifty or a hundred exceptional people together and let them perform with a minimal time investment from the rest of the organization? If so, your resources can be applied to other functions that will help you grow. It is a significant advantage to your business and your sanity.

The owner of an independent business or the general manager of a division is responsible for leading the people involved to a better use of resources. How you recruit and how you structure work will both matter, and you will have to set the tone and example. The next question will be how you manage individual people to help your business's growth, which is the subject of Chapter 9.

NOTES

1. This is the "85-15 rule": 85 percent of what goes wrong is with the system; the remainder, with an individual. For more, including examples, see Mary Walton's *Deming Management at Work* (New York: Perigee Books, 1990), p. 20. Also see W. Edwards Deming, *Out of the Crisis* (Cambridge, Mass.: MIT Press, 1986).
2. See Chapter 3, "What Keeps the CEO Up at Night?"
3. A shorter version of this discussion appeared in the article by Peter Meyer, "Trouble Finding Good People? Stop Trying to Hire Them," in *Business & Economic Review*, March 1998.
4. Conversation with the author, April 24, 1998.
5. Ann Winblad, "Leadership Secrets of a Venture Capitalist," *Leader to Leader* (Winter 1998), p. 12.
6. The people used as examples here are real Indies, but these are not their real names. If you want to contact one of them, please e-mail the author at Peter@MeyerGrp.com.
7. Winblad, "Leadership Secrets," p. 13.
8. Abraham Maslow identified a hierarchy of human needs that is often expressed as a pyramid—from basic-level needs to higher-level needs. It is his premise that once each of these needs has been satisfied, a person can go to the higher level. If the need recurs, the individual will return to that level until it is satisfied. The needs, from base level to top, are often expressed as: Psychological needs (hunger, thirst, etc.), Safety/Security (out of danger), Affiliation (being with oth-

ers), Esteem (to gain approval and recognition), and Self-Actualization.

9. For more on using the pyramid, see Chapter 9.
10. For a view of three different and complementary team designs, see Peter F. Drucker, *Managing in a Time of Great Change* (New York: Truman Talley Books/Plume, 1995), pp. 89–91.
11. If you wish to try this test yourself, I'd suggest that you contact Stave Puzzles, in Wilder, Vermont. It makes excellent puzzles for this purpose using guidelines that we created together.

CHAPTER NINE

Applications: Hire, Organize, Reward, and Keep Good People

If your business is to grow rapidly and sanely, you'll need more and more results from people. Salespeople need to generate more revenue this quarter than last. Purchasing needs to create and follow up on more deliveries this week than last. Production workers have to create more things to sell this year than last. People have limits—limits that the growth of an organization often stresses. They eventually run out of time to produce results. When people run out of time, it is your problem and theirs.

With rapid growth, it gets worse. You find that your business can't get enough people to create performance increases month over month. You can't even get enough people to do the work at the existing performance levels. Motivation is part of the answer at first. However, as W. Edwards Deming pointed out, exhortation cannot overcome failings in management and process. That makes them the concern of the owner or general manager.

Asking for more and more from people means that you find yourself spending more time on that resource. The business is investing one resource in another. This is reasonable but expensive.

Not all of the investment is in employees; you will invest time and money in many people who are outside the company as well. These are people your business relies on for growth, but they do not work for you in the classic sense. They will be suppliers, financiers, contractors, consultants, partners, and other people you may never see face-to-face. If you are growing a division, you will also have to invest time and money in internal suppliers and internal customers. Because your business is different from anything they work with now, the accounting, legal, and human resources teams will need your help to figure out how they can help you.

With gradual growth, you can plan for your people resources. With that plan, you can set aside time and money to hire and train the people you will need. Again, it is like building a high-rise office building. If you know that you will need ironworkers, you plan for them.

When the rate of growth picks up, your business loses access to the time and money that you need to get people on your staff. Instead, you hire outside companies and partner with others. You trade authority and control (and often more money) for speed, skill, and the flexibility to "fire" an outsider when you wish. Within the law, treat these people like every other person on whom you rely. Employee status is not a boundary to the person's need for guidance and support. Supporting nonemployees may be essential to achieve rapid growth for your business.

Many habits managers have developed cause them to invest in the past, not the future. Promotions, rewards, and reviews have been retrospective instruments. They can also be prospective tools to help your company grow sanely. Let's start with promotions.

Chart 9-1. Platform chart for sustainable warp-speed growth.

Chapter 12	Warp-Speed Growth: Managing a Business Built for Speed							
Chapters 7, 9, 11	APPLICATIONS ☞	Pricing	Tailoring	Prospective rewards	Indies	Prospective appraisals	Killer apps	Pain
Chapters 6, 8, 10	INVESTMENT STRATEGY ☞	Strategy—new markets		Strategy—recruiting and structure			Strategy—effect before technology (change is bad)	
Chapters 1–5	WHAT TO INVEST ☞	Time		People			Money	
	WHERE TO INVEST ☞	Create, dominate new markets		Technology			People	
	FOUNDATION ☞	Jigsaw management—Building a box top Deciding and communicating what to work on and what to let go						

WHY MAKE MANAGERS?

In the last chapter, I identified an opportunity to get more results from fewer managers by moving closer to an orchestral model. If you do this, you may have to change the way that you hand out promotions. Will that stop people from wanting these managerial spots? Will it stop your managers from wanting to develop new managers? Consider the following true story:

> Jane looked back at me and proceeded to ruin my whole day. We had planned the reorganization of our

division carefully, placing people in each place where they could make the most contribution. Jane saw that, but she wanted to be a manager instead.

When she had started with us, getting her management card punched was a major career step. We gave people increases in salary just for becoming a manager. As managers, we were rewarded for making more of ourselves. Management was a career step everyone focused on.

Since then, we have grown smarter. Should everyone be a manager? Not hardly. Should we all be developing managers? I think we know better now.

When Jane had started with us, proceeding to lead others in your skill was the next logical step. Then, it made sense. If you were good at something, and you could show others how to do it, we'd put you in charge of people who did the same thing. So salespeople became sales managers, engineers became vice presidents of engineering, financial analysts became controllers. It made sense if you needed people who were good at what their subordinates do.

Everything changes—so fast that the old structures get in the way. For instance, the technology changes faster than a manager can monitor and still focus on other tasks. The marketplace changes faster than management can cope with. The pace of financial change is intense enough to require ongoing attention from the best minds we have. Now, we need our best and brightest people on the front line. If they are truly expert, we can't afford the overhead of having them do something that they have not mastered.

We designed our reorganization with that principle in mind: The best people should do the work.

As their areas of expertise changed, our people quickly came to know more than their managers. Managers can never remain current. They will always be a step behind changes in the field. How much of a problem would that be? When we were honest with ourselves, we decided that this is nothing new.

Instead of trying to stretch the best people to be excellent at two things, we decided to eliminate the management roles. Who needs a manager who must always be updated on the latest changes? That simply slows us down and costs us time.

We asked, If someone is really the best at what he or she does, and knows what to do, does that person need a manager at all? The answer is yes. We don't need managers to supervise their old skill. We do need them to manage our resources wisely. That is another skill entirely.

Instead of making management a career step, we decided to make it a career. Then, we decided that it is a career that should get no more compensation or reward than any other. Clearly, some technical skills are worth even more to us than management skills. We started to compensate by skill set, not status.

This is not what Jane was thinking. She was concerned that we would hold her career back by not making her a manager. I told her all this. She was not convinced.

What did convince her was the way we now treat our individual contributors. We honor them to death. We pay them, of course, and well. But what really makes people want to do more work is to connect their contribution to their own sense of value, what Abraham Maslow called self-actualization. We do that religiously.

That is a skill only some people can do. We train for that skill just as we train salespeople to work their territory and technicians to test the hardware. This skill is what we call management. Managers are skill workers just like salespeople and engineers.

There are two critical skills. First, a manager working for us must be able to set a clear picture of what the other skill worker is to accomplish and then get out of the way. This is a delicate balance. It is showing a person the box top of the jigsaw puzzle without telling him or her how to assemble the pieces.

Second, our managers must know how to help individuals recognize their own contributions. This generally means that a good manager does not just tell the person how good he or she is; a good manager also helps an individual discover it himself or herself. To do this, we train good managers to talk less and ask many questions.[1]

The owner's or general manager's job? Develop those two skills and make sure they get honored at every level.

In the world of rapid growth, managers are skill workers, but at skills they do not yet have. You need to train, compensate, and honor managers—but no more and no less than you do engineers and salespeople. As you design management jobs around these skills, you may find a problem: You will have to change the criteria by which you do promote.

PROMOTIONS AND THE BUCKET OF ASHES

It is only a matter of time before the organization will put people into management slots. When you do, you must decide whether any of your people are the right candidates. A good decision on people will help you conserve time and grow in a sustainable manner. A poor choice can cripple your growth potential. This will happen for two reasons.

The first reason is results. That poor choice opens you to the probability that the results on which you rely will be late and/or poorly done. In a steady state, you can adapt. As the crush of growth increases, you have less flexibility, less room for a mistake in choosing managers.

The second reason is less obvious but even more critical. A poor choice will absorb your time and the time of the manager's team in making up for a bad decision. It is time that you cannot really afford if you want to make ever more aggressive targets. Poor management promotions can stunt growth.

When you promote a producer, will you hurt overall performance? Why do you promote one person over another, and how do you explain the reason?

The following true story illustrates a clean way to conserve both people and time for better investments:

> Jack sat down across from me, twenty days after I became his manager at IBM. He told me that he wanted me to promote him to a recently opened management slot. I asked him why. His reason was that he had put in three good years in this trench and had met his targets most of the time. He was looking for a reward.
>
> Vicki came to me the next day asking for the same promotion. Her first reason was that she was getting a little burned out and wanted a change. Vicki had been leading teams that were consistently top producers. We couldn't afford to lose her competency.[2]

Who gets the opportunity? Is promotion after a few years a reasonable expectation? Many people say it is. With reduced budgets, the pressure to use promotion as a reward for past behavior is stronger than ever. Consider an alternative. A best practice is to promote *prospectively* rather than *retrospectively.*

It's normal in most businesses to promote someone for two reasons:

1. Tenure (the person has the time in grade)
2. The need for a change (the person is burning out, but the manager wants to keep him or her in the organization)

If the person has done a good job for the organization, most companies will *reward* him or her with advancement. Most companies promote based on retrospective events, on what people have done in the past. It's an easy and satisfying way to deal with people, and it often works. As an example, consider Kent:

> Just after Jack and Vicki came to me, I got a new boss who had been promoted based on his history. Kent had been in the field earlier in his career and then became a very effective manager on staff. He came to us as a true star.
>
> In his new job with us, Kent got extensive on-the-

job training. All his OJT came from us, his subordinates. Kent worked hard, we worked hard, but he was
a fish out of water, and after sixty days, he was failing
miserably. This failure wasn't his fault. A person hired
for his or her past achievements is usually the wrong
person for the next job.

We took over the operation and made it run. Kent
didn't need to or get to do much. He did little damage
and was even twice given national recognition. Still,
we all knew it wasn't right. And word spread that he
was out of his depth and run by his team. That
stopped his advancement. Fair or not, others were not
willing to invest in a boss who was being managed by
events.

Kent, formerly a star for IBM, is now trying to rebuild his career. He could be a star again if someone
will take the time and effort to help him rebuild his
shattered self-image. He will probably retire first.[3]

What happens when the criteria for promotion are retrospective? Often, issues sort of work out. Either the new manager
gets trained, or he or she gets overrun by the people who are
supposed to be subordinates. Occasionally, the manager gets
blown out of the water by his or her own incompetence. You
will not know how bad the situation is until then. Of course,
then it is too late.

Getting trained (growing into the job) is what you hope for.
Otherwise, the employees can overrun the manager. That devas-
tates both the manager and the team. Such a team cannot deliver
the results the business needs to sustain growth.

When a manager's subordinates take time to train the manager, it reduces the amount of bandwidth available to create results for the business. If you have a great salesperson taking time
to whip a sales manager into shape, you lose opportunity. When
you miss opportunity, you have to change to a new market or
technology and try to catch up. You already face too much of
that as you grow. Asking that person to train your poor choice
as manager only makes the situation worse:

After three years, Kent was mercifully replaced with Bill. Bill, in his turn, had put in time on staff and was going to leave the company if he did not get a promotion. As a business, we were repeating the same mistake.

Promoting retrospectively, whether for time in grade or to keep the person from leaving, is common. It was killing our part of IBM.[4]

What other criteria for promotion are there besides time in grade and the need to keep the person from leaving? I suggest prospective performance, following what I call the Carl Sandburg school of management. Prospective performance looks at what the person will do for you in the future. Retrospective performance is like Sandburg's comment that "the past is a bucket of ashes." Historical past events are not the correct way to build a manager for the future:

I didn't explain this to Jack and Vicki. I was in a hurry to grow the business. Instead, I asked them what they each considered criteria for promotion.

Jack felt that promotion should come from past performance and loyalty. He asked about my own experience, and I even told him the truth. (My first management job came from surviving attrition.) Vicki told me that she wasn't ready for management yet but had it as a goal. She felt that she could do the job well for the company and that the company would benefit if we promoted her.

I told them each that I had only one criterion, and that was whether the candidate would do the future job exceptionally well. The past might be an indicator, but we cannot treat the future of our organizations as though we are phoenixes, flying backward to see where we come from. Jack did not like that answer. He was still looking for promotion as a reward.

Jack did not get the promotion. We took care of him by assigning him to a team where he could be a real contributor and make a lot of money. He never understood the reasoning but accepted the money and satisfaction.

Vicki, who focused on the future, is one of the best managers in the division. She may wind up over-running Bill any day now. Neither of us could be more pleased. No manager can do any better than to pro-mote into success, not from it. That is the difference between the past being a bucket of ashes and making the future into one.[5]

USING INCENTIVES TO HELP GROWTH

Rewards are an investment in your business—again, measured in time, people, and money. As with promotions, rewards usu-ally focus on past behavior. However, the purpose of rewards is to improve the business for the future, and with rapid growth, you don't really have time to focus solely on the past. A better practice is to use rewards prospectively and leverage your time, people, and money.[6]

In the mid-1990s, BigTel was growing so rapidly that it could not hire fast enough to feed the growth.[7] The stress of never having enough people generated strain for every depart-ment. Mark, a second-level manager running an order-fulfill-ment operation, raised a problem that was typical at the time: "How can I get better rewards for less? I know that I can get more business results from rewards. We need more rewards to keep people going. We have less money for rewards. We want the rewards to lead directly to more performance. Is there a bet-ter answer?"

When you have an opportunity to reward, take advantage of the following model, which Mark used at BigTel.

The Principle of Using Rewards to Motivate

Mark's order-fulfillment operation was a support function with little glamour but high value. He and the team knew that BigTel could not grow without his team's doing a great job. Nonethe-less, they felt unappreciated.

As is typical of fast growth, nine-tenths of Mark's people had been in the job less than a year. As is typical of many organizations, most of Mark's people had one career manager but reported to at least two different people for their day-to-day work. In structuring his reward program, Mark used all these factors as advantages.

He changed the normal emphasis on money to an emphasis on motivators. This required four specific steps:

1. Mark re-created Maslow's hierarchy of human needs in words that his managers would use every day. If you do this, ask your managers to pick the words that matter. As Maslow had done, Mark drew this as a pyramid. (See Figure 9-1.)

2. He brainstormed as many reward ideas as he could. (See Figure 9-2 for a sample list.)

3. He assigned each reward idea to one level in the hierarchy. Rewards at the top of the pyramid are the most meaningful to both the person and the company.

4. He chose to use the rewards that belonged at the top levels of the pyramid and would also contribute prospectively to the business. In other words, instead of rewarding just for past behavior, Mark and his managers rewarded prospectively as

Figure 9-1. Mark's hierarchy of needs.

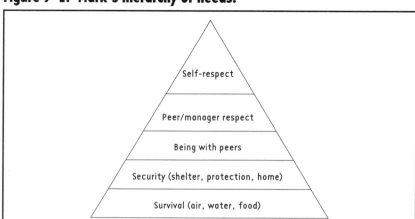

Self-respect

Peer/manager respect

Being with peers

Security (shelter, protection, home)

Survival (air, water, food)

Figure 9-2. List of great inexpensive rewards.

Management Team's List of Effective and Inexpensive Rewards

—Raises and bonuses
—Social functions
—Outings
—A night on the town
—A nice meal or lunch on the manager
—A group lunch for which the manager pays
—Dinner
—A pizza party
—Picnics for teams
—Golf or other sporting events in which both team members and
  managers participate
—Direct praise
—Peer recognition
—Letters of recognition, either kept on file or displayed where
  customers can see them
—Broadcasting of customer compliments and commendations in voice
  mail or writing
—Written praise from the branch
—One-on-one verbal praise
—Day off or time off
—Cash
—Tickets to sporting events, ballet, and so forth that people attend
  by themselves
—Certificates and plaques
—Shirts, phones, pins, hats, cups, and so on, all imprinted with the
  name of the company
—A parking space
—Additional responsibilities
—Opportunities to excel
—Additional training
—A personal call from the senior executive of the company
—Better tools
—People allowed to bid on projects they would most prefer

well. They rewarded with tools to help move the business forward.

This approach makes each reward both retrospective (recognizing past behavior) and prospective (helping sustain growth).

To replicate this process, ask your team to follow the same steps. Create a pyramid in which the levels of the hierarchy are expressed in your own terms. (I have noted the terms we used with Mark's team.) Then list all of your existing and potential rewards. Assign each reward to the appropriate level of the hierarchy. Start using rewards that are at the top of the pyramid instead of at the bottom.

Levels 1 and 2—Basic Requirements

Level 1 of Mark's hierarchy of needs (the base of the pyramid) is to provide basic physical living requirements such as food and shelter. Level 2 is to provide stability and security for the person and his or her family. These were issues in Mark's department. The pace of work caused his people to miss time at home and with their families. Although money and dinners are common rewards in most organizations, Mark quickly determined that, for his team, their reward value should be rated at no higher than level 2.

Level 3—Being with Peers

The next level up on the hierarchy is to be with people. This level recognizes that people are motivated to join, just to be with others. Mark's people reported to other departments for day-to-day direction. Mark turned this to his advantage.

He structured interaction with more field people to be a reward, not a duty. Entry level for Mark's people included little field interaction. As the person grew in the job, the manager increased that interaction. The person identified more fully with that group. This improved his or her feelings about the work, which in turn improved results for Mark and the company.

Level 4—Peer Recognition

Mark and his managers immediately improved their definition of peers. Peers are not just other people at the same level. Peers include contacts beyond the immediate team—suppliers and customers and others both within and outside the parent company. And what about the manager to whom that person is supposed to report? Mark realized that managers are never more than peers.

Mark carefully planned recognition. When a person did an outstanding job, Mark made sure a local manager recognized him or her in front of the peers who got the most benefit, the group that will show their appreciation in the clearest manner. If the peers were in Boston, the person flew to Boston, and the highest manager available recognized the contributor in front of the peers. Mark found that the excitement generated more than repaid the investment in time and travel. The recognized employee came back wanting to work even harder for those peers who got the benefit.

Level 5—More Success through Self-Recognition

Maslow refers to self-actualization, but Mark thought in terms of what happens when a person recognizes himself or herself for excelling. Nothing stays with a person longer than his or her self-image, which makes self-recognition a wonderful reward. This reward needn't cost much and needn't take much of the manager's time. It does take a valuable skill—the ability to ask a question to which you know the answer and let someone else answer it.

For example, when Mark did peer recognition at an event, he asked the person to explain how he or she did the task that earned the reward. By asking the person to recognize his or her own actions, Mark helped the individual move to the top of the pyramid. An extra bonus for the organization is that the person's peers are learning at the same time.

The next step is to connect the reward to the work. Growth creates a never-ending stream of new tasks coming up, and Mark offered to let his best people bid on those tasks as a reward. The way to get the best new project was to earn it.

Consider allowing your people to bid on a tool or a project or a customer instead of a task. Will your office be getting a new computer? Why not give it to a person who will excel with it and wants the next opportunity to feel good about his or her work? It helps the person, it helps the company, and it saves you time. The reward becomes prospective while it recognizes the past.

Eventually, your best people start to work more for themselves. They do it for a reward program that adds little cost to your budget and delivers more enthusiasm and skill to the work at hand. You will have started to change the nature of the work and free up more resources for growth.

CAN APPRAISALS HELP GROWTH?

Despite the value of time, let me suggest four reasons to invest it in appraisals:

1. Everyone likes to know how he or she is doing.
2. The cliché "What gets inspected gets expected" is true. If you say something is important but don't check on it, you are implying that it really wasn't.
3. If appraisals are done well, they will improve performance quickly, fueling growth.
4. If done well, they can help your people grow more quickly. You'll need this for growth.

If all that is true, two questions remain:

1. Why don't companies get better results from doing appraisals?
2. How do we change appraisals to make them good tools for rapid growth?

Don't Annual Appraisals Work?

In a landmark study, a group of managers at General Electric asked, "Why don't annual appraisals work?" and did the research, surveys, and analysis to answer the question.[8] My firm repeated the study, on a smaller scale, at a multinational non-profit organization in 1995 with the same results. The studies found that most managers and employees think that appraisals are a good idea. Both studies also showed what most managers will tell you: Appraisals are rarely done on time and completely. There is considerable reluctance to do annual appraisals in most North American organizations. That reluctance is understandable: The way most companies do them, appraisals can hurt the company's ability to perform. The following list shows how.

Effects of Traditional Appraisals on Organizations

- Criticism has a negative effect on performance.
- Praise has little effect on performance, either positive or negative.
- Performance improves most when the manager and employee establish specific goals.
- Most people feel disconnected from goals that are set for them.
- Mutual goal setting improves performance.
- Employee participation in appraisals drops if appraisals are conducted annually. Doing appraisals other than annually improves performance.

And it is not hard to understand why appraisals have these effects. Each year, managers spend countless hours focusing on the exact words they want to use to explain the compensation and coach better performance. The person being appraised wonders how a full year of events, results, failures, and successes can fit meaningfully into such a small form. He or she especially wonders how that will play out in terms of compensation.

After the hours spent wordsmithing (time not spent growing the business), the manager carefully discusses the entire past year and the entire next year. What does the employee hear? The one sentence with the percentage or dollars in it.

The discussion of performance is necessarily broad and feels disconnected from what actually happened during the year. It is rarely participative, usually one-sided. All of this makes it acutely uncomfortable for both parties. None of this is likely to help growth.

Building a Better Appraisal Process

Bonnie Nunke, former VP of human resources for Compression Laboratories, Inc. (CLI),[9] wanted to provide a truly useful decision and appraisals tool. Nunke wanted CLI's managers to integrate appraisals into everyday work. "Performance appraisals are a system, not an event," she notes. The appraisal process "goes on all year, it needs constant attention."[10]

To make this easier for them, Nunke showed the team how to use the jigsaw management model from Chapter 2 to build an ongoing appraisal process that would be better for the company and its people. In the rest of this subsection, I explain what she did. Later in this chapter, I present steps you can take to emulate Nunke's approach.

She asked the managers to look for the borders of an individual project. She counseled them to define success clearly and in advance. Nunke knew this would cause a discussion of which pieces belonged in the individual project (or puzzle, as she called it) and which did not. These conversations built a framework for operational decisions and formed borders within which to work. As Nunke pointed out, "You never know if the piece you left out was what the individual thought was most important." The only way to find out is to work to the same image. Defining success criteria for the results, not the process to reach the results, made both appraisers and those being appraised much more comfortable.

The managers used the box top to start tying appraisals to projects and events, not to the calendar. The result was an ongoing process of continual appraisals, not "something you pull out once a year and dust off." By doing appraisals for every project, the managers were helping define the projects before they started, helping to ensure that people spent less time on extraneous pieces. This process built a better project and a better appraisal. For the growing business, this delivers the result in less time with the same (or fewer) people.

This happened as Nunke encouraged her appraisers to set

the annual process aside for the time being and start doing informal, conversational, project-based appraisals. Each appraiser would set up a sort of miniappraisal to be done at the end of the project. This was specific to the one project and would evaluate performance against the success criteria set up for that project. Without stating it, Nunke was asking her teams to change the nature of the work from measured process to measured results.

This sponsored faster change because the manager and employee (or Indy) could start any corrections at once, not at the end of the year. Performance improvements might take effect six or nine months sooner, a considerable difference to a rapidly growing company.

Because the discussions took place in the immediate context of the work, and because managers did not link salary to these conversations, the process was much easier on everyone. The manager and employee focused and agreed on performance issues. Then they scored the employee's performance, noted the score, and set it aside.

At the end of the compensation year, the manager could sit down with the employee, and they would review the records of the performances. Since criticism and congratulations had already been expressed, the process is objective and free of surprises. If the manager chose to score projects on a scale of 1 to 10, it would be as simple as, "You scored 80 percent across all these projects. That is good, and you'll get an X percent raise."

Putting the Guidelines into Action

When you sit down to create an appraisal, start by building the edges of the puzzle, with the success criteria of the specific assignment. Since these are ongoing appraisals, make these the success criteria for the exact project you have in mind. (To define success criteria, look for answers to questions like the examples shown in Figure 9-3.) The answers define borders, ruling activities out of the project. This will save time, people, and money. If the project is too big for crisp success criteria, break it into chunks small enough to define neatly.

One piece of the picture may be the checkpoints that you want to include. The checkpoints are where you can see whether

Figure 9-3. Example questions to help design jigsaw management appraisal.

The Borders:
Is this more than one project?
When is the project due?
What will have changed when the project is done?
What constraints must be honored?

The Picture:
What tools will you use to measure success? How often will you use them?
What people, money, and other resources will you need?
How will we define interim progress?
When should we meet to check and review progress?

the person is wandering outside the borders or missing a piece of the puzzle that he or she should not.

You can start the review as soon as the project is over by simply asking, "Did we meet the success criteria we set?" and then, "Did we go outside the boundaries we started with?" I would suggest that you agree on a specific scoring system, such as ranking the desired results from 1 to 10. If you find that you want to add a result or skill, do so in the next project.

Because you conducted checkpoints at regular intervals, there are few surprises. Because you have been discussing results regularly, you can ask the person to rate his or her recent performance. Then you can do what's really valuable: You can focus on the future, not the past. The future is where improvement can happen.

Six Steps to Use a Results-Oriented Appraisal Process

The results-oriented appraisal process works with any manager who is supervising any employee or Indy. The process consists of the following six steps, which are actually easier to do than to describe:

1. Ask the employee or Indy you are appraising if it will be okay to track the work, so that you can tell how events are going

and keep everything on track. Make it clear that these notes are not for corporate files but just for you and the person.

2. Ask questions like those shown in Figure 9-3. Write the answers down. Show them to the other person and ask whether any correction is needed. If you think the targets are too aggressive, ask whether you can back off on them. This information goes into a desk file (physical or electronic) that does not become part of the corporate personnel files. You'll pull out this file when you do an interim or final review of the project.

3. Meet again at a reasonable check-in time. Ask for an update. Then ask the person how he or she is doing against the original specs. If the targets need to be changed, change them. The point is not to hold the person to the original list; it is to have a realistic plan that moves the business forward.

4. When the project is done, or a major checkpoint is reached, ask the employee or Indy to evaluate his or her performance. Evaluate it yourself. Discuss the performance and grade it right there. Never delay feedback; just take the time to give correction when it is going to be most useful for you both—at the checkpoint. When you appraise immediately, you often get two effects.The first is that people are harder on themselves than you might be. If so, correct expectations and move on. The second effect is that if a person thinks the task is unfair or undoable, he or she will tell you right then and there. If so, now is the time to deal with it.

5. Write up the project or checkpoint appraisal within a day, copying the person who was appraised. Go on to the next project or checkpoint and repeat the appraisal process.

6. When it comes time to hold a salary discussion, take out the desk file. This will tell both you and the employee or Indy what is fair. If performance has been good, it will be shown in the file and there will be little to argue over. This uncouples the appraisal process from the salary discussion. That means you can get improvements in results without waiting to increase a salary.

The rule of thumb for appraisals has been that you did them once a year for all employees, with each review covering the entire preceding year. The rule for a business going through rapid growth is to do appraisals at least every six weeks and with any person on whom you rely. These are prospective reviews, which help build the future and promote sustainable growth.

When you decide that you value resources and design your business to invest them wisely, many processes will change. Beyond promotions, rewards, and appraisals (the examples discussed here), how your business manages people one on one can be a tool to grow rapidly without growing out of control.

NOTES

1. The names have been changed. This story is adapted from an article by Peter Meyer, "Why Make Managers?" *Business Horizons*, January 1996.
2. Although the company name is real, the names of the people have been changed. The information is taken in adapted form from two articles, both by Peter Meyer: "Promotions Are Not a Reward—Manager's Journal," *Wall Street Journal*, May 1, 1995, and "Successful Promotions and the Bucket of Ashes," *Business Horizons*, May 1994.
3. Ibid.
4. Ibid.
5. Ibid.
6. The material in this section appeared in a different form in an article by Peter Meyer, "Effective Incentives," *Solutions*, November 1995.
7. The case is real, but the company's and person's names have been changed.
8. Meyer, Kay, and John R. P. French, "Split Roles in Performance Reviews," *Harvard Business Review*, January 1965.
9. Now a subsidiary of VTEL Corporation.
10. This discussion is adapted from an article by Peter Meyer, "Jigsaw Management: Piecing Together Appraisals," *Solutions*, June 1995.

Chapter Ten

Resource Strategies: Growth and Technology

We usually equate advanced technology and automation with speed and progress. Technology can be a tool to get more done in less time, a force for good. It works that way on the television spaceship I mentioned in the Introduction, but it does not always work that way in real life. Technologies are neutral. They can help your business grow, or they can help you spiral down into an expensive crater. How your business uses them determines which of those experiences you will have.

If your critical resources are time, people, and money, will technologies help you manage them? The key is not the answer (the technologies) but getting the question right.

To make growth sustainable and sane, you should be managing it, not vice versa. Technology is one of the best places in which you can invest time, people, and money. Chapters 10 and 11 discuss wise investment strategies and some example applications. A wise investment strategy and applications often mean doing less than you might think or even nothing at all.

Chart 10-1. Platform chart for sustainable warp-speed growth.

Chapter 12	*Warp-Speed Growth: Managing a Business Built for Speed*								
Chapters 7, 9, 11	APPLICA-TIONS ☞	Pricing	Tailoring	Prospective rewards	Indies	Prospective appraisals	Killer apps	Pain
Chapters 6, 8, 10	INVEST-MENT STRATEGY ☞	Strategy—new markets		Strategy—recruiting and structure			Strategy—effect before technology (change is bad)	
Chapters 1–5	WHAT TO INVEST ☞	Time		People			Money	
	WHERE TO INVEST ☞	Create, dominate new markets		Technology			People	
	FOUNDA-TION ☞	*Jigsaw management—Building a box top Deciding and communicating what to work on and what to let go*							

HOW MUCH DOES THAT TECHNOLOGY *REALLY* COST YOUR GROWING BUSINESS?

The good news is that the new technologies your business bought are already in the hands of those who can use them best—your line employees. The bad news is the investment. The real cost is probably larger than you ever dreamed possible. Whereas most businesses look at the dollar cost of new technologies, rapidly growing companies have to look not only at the investment of money involved but also at the investment of time and people. To understand the real costs that you are incurring, you should start with the effect you want to create.[1]

Looking at effect first is difficult, especially for companies that promote innovation in their own marketing. It requires that you challenge your own thoughts on the advantages of innovation and start with the idea that change is bad.

If change is bad, why do it? You would certainly not change your business just to use a technology. You would change only to get some far better effect that the technology helps deliver. Have you ever acquired new computer software or hardware only to discover that the software isn't what you expected, the changes are hard to get used to, and the tools are in all the wrong places? These changes are disruptive: They cost you time and take your people away from what they should be doing.

So why bother? The only reason to invest in that disruption is to get some great effect that a new package offers. Most of us only have to upgrade a computer once to decide that change for technology's sake does not promote sane growth.

However, what is going on in your growing company or division while you are reading this?

- ✢ Someone is buying the latest class of personal computers.
- ✢ Someone is looking into network computing.
- ✢ Someone is attending a seminar, learning how to build you an *intra*net to go with your Internet.
- ✢ Someone is choosing a numerical control or database marketing system. With luck, no one will try to explain it to you later.
- ✢ Someone is buying a copier that has more computing

Figure 10-1. Always start with the assumption that change is bad.

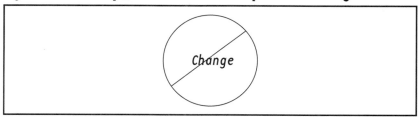

power than your entire school had when you got your degree.
✧ Someone is losing at a computer game that would have overloaded the big computer you bought a few years ago.

What is costing you is the *time* your people spend on selecting, implementing, and learning to use technology. The hardware is cheap. Software is almost, but not quite, cheap. Support is still inexpensive. Although these are the costs that get the attention when most executives think of technologies, they are far from the greatest expense for growing companies.

From the perspective of using your resources wisely, your people's time and focus are likely to provide your competitive advantage next year, not the new computers. The hardware costs are small. If your line teams buy only half the tools they are looking at, you will spend more in opportunity costs than you want to calculate. That is the danger of new technologies.

THE PRICE OF TECHNOLOGY EMPOWERMENT

Letting users choose their own technology is a recent phenomenon. A few years ago, companies had an information technology (IT) department with experts who spoke their own language. You could rely on them to design technology investments so that they made sense for your business. They delivered the tools to your people when and where needed. Or so you hoped.

Using the IT department had a big advantage: It put the process of choosing and buying technology into the hands of people who were trained to understand what IP (Internet Protocol) is and who had the time to investigate why a photocopier might need to use it. That meant that your sales managers sold, your operations managers made things happen, and your finance people made sure you were in control. But IT lost credibility with many business functions when it seemed to put technology ahead of business functions.

Today, every department can have its own informal IT function. Your most critical people manage the local area networks (LANs), support the database application, and make sure that the clients and servers keep their roles straight. The line team supplies that IT function. The cost to be concerned with is not hardware and software. Your business should be most concerned with the opportunity cost you incur when your best people do IT work.

Time is your most critical resource, the one you can never regain. When your best people spend it in the wrong place, your business slows. When your best frontline resources are focusing on which Netscape plug-in to install, your growing company is getting slower. You are not losing opportunities because you are getting *more* bureaucratic but because you are getting *less* so.

One response is to speed up your activities in order to recapture the opportunities, to try and do it all. This leads to spinning out of control. Instead, let's look at putting effect ahead of technology in your products and operations.

PUTTING EFFECT AHEAD OF TECHNOLOGY IN YOUR PRODUCTS

A clear example comes from 3Com's Palm Computing Division. When 3Com bought U.S. Robotics in 1997, the company acquired the PalmPilot product line. A handheld computer (also called a PDA, or personal digital assistant), the PalmPilot is designed to replace the organizer books that many people carry around to track schedules, phone numbers, and expenses. Beyond organizing your time, you can get software that allows you to use your PalmPilot to do anything from games to e-mail to construction estimating.

PDAs have been available for years. Companies such as Apple (the Newton), Sharp, Casio, Sony, and IBM have delivered PDAs. All but one have failed to sell to expectations; some have been spectacular mistakes. The first (and so far only) product to achieve market acceptance is the Palm.

What is unique about the Palm line is that it sells well. It works in the market. A little more than a year after its introduction, there were about twice as many Palm brand products in use as all the other products *combined*. Perhaps the major contributor to this success is how the designers made sure that creeping elegance would not kill the product's growth.

They did it by setting a box top for the PalmPilot and insisting on sticking to that vision. This resulted from deep involvement as software providers for the early PDAs. Watching the failures convinced Jeff Hawkins (Palm Computing's original president) and his team that the early proponents were putting much too much emphasis on technology and too little on effect.

While the people developing PDAs were adding features, PalmPilot's team leaders stuck to four success criteria, which they would not negotiate:

1. The PalmPilot had to be small enough to be "thoughtlessly" portable.

2. It had to communicate seamlessly with a personal computer—to act as an accessory, not as a replacement. (The idea was that buyers would not want to have two separate computers but would like a device that would extend the function to pocket or purse.)

3. The system had to be fast and simple. (Palm's primary competition would be the organizers that professionals already carried around, not PCs.)

4. The PalmPilot had to sell for less than $300 (U.S.).

The effect they delivered was low technology. The tool was fast, simple, and it turned on as soon as you touched the power button. Pressure to add more computer features was intense, but the PDA manufacturers that had failed remained excellent examples of the dangers of creeping elegance. In an interview with David Gewirtz in *PalmPower*, Hawkins noted that people came to him to "say, 'Oh, why don't you build something that's tablet size or a Newton size?' " He would respond, "You know, there may be a market there but you have to know what you're going after and that's not it for us."[2] As the company grew, Hawkins emphasized that this focus is part of the "core knowledge" that each Palm Computing employee must learn. The market does not reward the latest advances. Trying to deliver technological elegance for its own sake is a sure way to fail.

Besides ensuring that the device would be more marketable, this box top enabled the company to get the product to market more quickly. The focus on the four success criteria made it possible to skip past hundreds of decisions on how to design add-ons, how to run Windows CE, and how to build other features that would not quite fit into the box top. Instead of designing interfaces for printing, the team got the machine ready to ship at the right time to become immensely popular.

Although other personal digital assistants had considerable flexibility and a Windows operating system, PalmPilot is inexpensive and uncomplicated. It turns out that this simplicity, not added technology or features, is the effect that people will pay for. The added features of Windows or the Newton were an investment of resources that actually hurt market acceptance.

PUTTING EFFECT AHEAD OF TECHNOLOGY IN YOUR OPERATIONS

In late 1997, the Federal Deposit Insurance Corporation (FDIC) faced a similar decision. The recent health of banks and savings and loans in the United States allowed the corporation's Division of Finance (DOF) to set aside a substantial amount of money for computers for 1998. Despite the substantial funds, the executives felt sure that the demand for that money would exceed the supply. The chief financial officer (CFO) and director of finance, Paul Sachtlaben, asked whether the executives could rank the expenditures around a plan. Specifically, he did not want a technology plan but rather a plan for what the investments would deliver in terms of effect. This raised a problem. Most of the executive staff did not agree on what they wanted the technology to deliver. Managers suggested many great ideas but no way to decide what constituted a great way to spend the tens of millions of dollars.

The FDIC, like most large organizations, has a substantial professional information technology group, called the Division of Information Resource Management, or DIRM. DIRM was ready to spend the money. Managers in the DOF were also ready to spend. Sachtlaben wanted to know whether that money was going to be well spent. The issue was that no one had defined *well spent.*

Solving the FDIC's problem may seem like an easy exercise.

Most managers can compile a list of technologies that they want. However, all that produces is a list of technologies. It does not screen for the effects a business needs.

For example, in 1997, there was a discussion in the IT industry about whether to go to NT workstations or stick with UNIX. It might be a hot technical debate, but the results are not what Sachtlaben was interested in.

Fred Selby, the deputy director who ran management services for Sachtlaben, stopped to ask the right question: Did Sachtlaben want to decide what *technologies* to buy or what *effects* to buy? Selby started asking for a set of principles by which he could judge a good investment. And the more he talked about it, the more clear it became that advanced technology would not be the right criterion for a good investment. The effect that the technology supports would justify the investment.

Selby and Sachtlaben wanted a list of system principles, guidelines that they could pass on to all the managers. These guidelines would tell the managers what to look for in a system that deserved funding. Because very little in the way of work can be done without technology, these guidelines might have to apply to almost every project being considered. The guidelines would go to the first-line managers, so that they could implement them early in a project, before a great deal of time and people got invested. The guidelines would help the managers to focus on the effect first and let the technology groups decide how to deliver it.

But what effect did the division want? Selby and Sachtlaben asked our firm to come in and pose the same question to the other executives and then get the senior management team to give clear answers. It was a difficult change in mind-set for many. When the team members came together to agree on what effects they wanted, it took a day and a half of additional discussion. The list of answers surprised them.

The process delivered the two lists in Figure 10-2—a list of general requirements and a list of technical requirements. Some were specific to the FDIC, but most were not. These can be used by any business.

These lists look clear now, but they were quite difficult to create and understand for many people in the room. The FDIC

Figure 10-2. FDIC system principles.

FDIC SYSTEM PRINCIPLES

General and System Principles

General Principles

General Principle #1: CLIENT NEEDS

Business Processes and the systems that support them exist to meet the needs of our clients. Therefore, their design must be guided by an understanding of the needs of our clients, and our clients must be involved in the entire system development process, from the design of specifications through user testing and implementation.

General Principle #2: CORPORATE FOCUS

The systems that DOF operates and the data those systems contain are Corporate:

The Division of Finance is the steward of those systems and data.

The Corporate stakeholders in the systems and data have to buy into their design and operation.

Generally, all data and information will be made available to anyone in the Corporation unless there is a sound business reason for restricting access to it.

General Principle #3: DATA INTEGRITY

The DOF systems ensure that the data collected reflect the substance of the accountable event, that it is collected contemporaneously with the Accountable Event. The data will be edited and validated within the DOF system.

General Principle #4: PROCESS FOCUS

Systems development begins with a review and documentation of the business process of which it is a part. Part of this review is a preliminary cost/benefit analysis that addresses the improvements expected in the efficiency and effectiveness of the process.

(continues)

Figure 10-2. *(continued)*

General Principle #5: DATA CONSISTENCY

Data are maintained only once in a single system of record. While data may be replicated for different purposes, the replicas will always be synchronized with the original.

General Principle #6: AUDIT TRAIL

All data must be clearly and easily traceable to its underlying accountable event.

General Principle #7: POLICY CONSTRAINTS

All Business Processes and their supporting systems must conform to applicable corporate policies and legislative or regulatory requirements.

General Principle #8: SYSTEM IMPACTS

Business Processes and their supporting systems cannot be modified without considering the impact of the modification on other processes, systems, or organizations.

General Principle #9: HISTORICAL CONSTRAINTS

The redesign of Business Processes and supporting systems should be based on a fresh examination of how to most effectively and efficiently meet the needs of our clients.

System Principles

System Principle #1: SOURCE OF INFORMATION

Systems should support users providing data.

System Principle #2: AUDIT TRAIL

Systems should allow reconstruction of a transaction.

System Principle #3: DATA LOCATION

The General Ledger is the source of summary data; the subsidiary ledger is the source of detail.

Figure 10-2. *(continued)*

System Principle #4: SYSTEM CONTROL

A change control and operational balancing mechanism must be in place to ensure orderly modification and operation of systems.

System Principle #5: CUSTOMIZATION

Minimize customization through knowledge of our vendors, our IT environment, and our applications.

System Principle #6: CREEPING ELEGANCE

Avoid creeping elegance.

System Principle #7: DATA ENTRY

There should be a single point of entry for each piece of data.

System Principle #8: DATA TYPES

Reporting tools will not access production data.

System Principle #9: DATA CONSISTENCY

One term means the same thing throughout the division (data dictionary issue). Standardization of terms throughout the Corporation will be coordinated with DIRM.

System Principle #10: SDLC

Follow the Systems Development Lifecycle Methodology

---

was not accustomed to asking users what they wanted. Most CFOs have a staff that has fallen into the habit of telling users what they must do to meet legal and procedural requirements. The first general principle suggested that Sachtlaben's team could not do that. Instead, the management team would have to learn to "sell" the functions and value to other divisions that would have to use the tools. Sachtlaben and his immediate staff were asking the managers to put the effect the users needed *before* the technology the Division of Finance wanted.

Sachtlaben's team asked the managers and individual contributors to work with end users to define success for an investment. To do this, the manager and individual contributors first define the success criteria, and then the manager and end users add the lists of general principles and system principles to the criteria. This generates the limited options passed to the technology experts in the Division of Finance and DIRM. Then the technology groups recommend the appropriate platforms and software. Although the money saved on technology is substantial, the real return is much higher. It starts with the time saved.

The managers no longer have to deal with how to implement a technology until they are sure that they will use that technology. They save tens or hundreds of person-months in training, design, and planning. Because fewer technologies get tried and then abandoned, the infrastructure costs to support computers go down as well. Finally, the rework necessary to adapt the technology to the users is cut substantially. Time and people savings are enormous.

The benefits flow beyond Sachtlaben's direct team. When the effect is put first, the user communities spend less time on technology issues that change rapidly and more time on their real work. They also invest less time in rework and in trying to adapt a technology to what they do and have to get done. Instead, the design for technology use is done up front, and the user community can put that technology to work more quickly.

The technologists prefer this approach as well. By giving DIRM the success criteria without defining the tools to produce the effect, the Division of Finance gives the experts the room to do what they do best. DIRM still has to convince the finance managers that it is recommending the right solution, but the argument gets easier for both. Instead of discussing whether NT is inherently better than UNIX, they are discussing which system delivers the limited solutions the users actually need.

The users wind up with a better solution. Applying the principles in Figure 10-2 often causes a useful discussion between the users and the FDIC financial community. An idea that makes sense on its own merits may conflict with other ongoing efforts. The manager will modify it to meet the relevant system principles. As that happens, the plan becomes less elegant and more realistic. Always, the box top guides the design. If the teams follow the box top, the effect is the key to any decisions.

Benefits Accrued by Putting Effect Ahead of Technology

- ✧ The financial savings are substantial.
- ✧ Less time is required to learn and adopt new systems.
- ✧ Less time is required for training.
- ✧ Less time is required to rework implementations.
- ✧ Systems are easier for users to access and operate.
- ✧ Technologists focus on what they do best.
- ✧ Users get a better solution.
- ✧ The right tools are available sooner.

During the process of defining the guidelines, two road-blocks stood out. The first was enforcement. No one knew quite where the final decision to invest rested. Once the managers had a clear document to follow for defining a project, to whom did they send recommendations? Who could finally say yes or no?

The second roadblock was how to get meaningful end-user interaction. The team intuitively knew that a CEO's staff cannot always dictate what to do. Nor can it just go ask, "What do you want?" and hope to get meaningful answers.

Sachtlaben ensured that both concerns were addressed. For the first, he asked the top executives below him to declare very loudly that they make decisions as a group. He asked them to say no often enough to show that they would enforce the new standards.

The second barrier, interaction, is more difficult. You cannot mandate intelligent interaction and questioning. You have to de-velop a methodology for people who do not normally do these things. Your methodology has to help the team learn to question users and draw out the key requirements, even if users have not thought about them.

All this put and kept the emphasis on the effect instead of on the technology. It made the FDIC's technology-acquisition process both easier to start and easier to live with. FDIC employ-ees now have more time in their week to do the real work of the FDIC.

Implementing This Approach in a Growing Business

To keep the business moving faster and faster, you want to leave responsibility and authority at the front line. The answer to how to invest properly in technology isn't centralization, nor is it returning to refrigerator-sized computers that require water to cool them and gurus to run them. You don't want a technical solution, nor do you want to ask each manager to bring the technology decisions to you. Instead, ask the line to buy effect instead of technology.

Consider your best salespeople as a model. You probably ask your sales teams to sell the sizzle, not the steak. Your best people sell what the *user* gets and does. That effect for the user becomes the compelling reason to buy your features and benefits. A great salesperson focuses on effect before process or tools. It's more customer-centered, and it works.

Ask your line people to treat investments in technology the same way. They should buy *what* the device does for the user, not *how* it does it. As with the FDIC and with PalmPilot, ask your managers to buy for the user and avoid creeping elegance. Here are two steps to consider:

1. Require the line people looking at a new technology to define the consumer of that technology. It's the first question to look at, before the processor or the price. Whether the technology is a copier or an intranet, is Herm down the hall the person who will benefit? If so, forget the folks on the other floor; focus on Herm and his peers.

2. Ask your people to define the effect as their customer sees it. What does Herm need? Will this technology provide it?

Asking about the technology itself is not the role of the general manager or owner. The senior executive's role is to make sure that someone is asking about the effect and whether the technology meets the needs of the users.

If you are the senior executive, an effective role is to tell your people that you will let them study and buy *anything* that they think makes sense. All you ask in return is that when you wander down to Herm, he can show that he is more effective than he used to be, that he can say the disruption has been worth his time.

If he is and can, then you will be happy. Tell your managers that if Herm is not substantially more effective—no matter how modern the product or technology, no matter how good the deal—the manager who imposed the technology goes to the head of the line for new opportunities in northern Manitoba.

WHAT IS THE COST OF FREE?

That "free" set of features may cost you more than you ever thought possible. In the old days, when new technology came with additional features that no one knew how to use, your IT department would figure out what to do with them. Now, who will study those features? It will be your best people, taking time away from your core work. If you want wise growth, you cannot afford that.

When your line people invest in technological overkill, they are trading present time for future value. That decision is usually unconscious. Consider: How often do you allow your finance people to trade present value for future value without thinking it through? Here, the cost is time away from key tasks. Don't let your best people unconsciously spend your most critical resource. Direct them to avoid buying futures that do not have a clear benefit to Herm or his equivalent.

Giving the Right Direction

The task of the owner or general manager is to set the structure and define the work. Even if network computers sound suspiciously like the unintelligent terminals that IBM used to sell you, don't spend time on that. Worry about what your line people are doing with their time. If they are improving the effect of what you deliver, forget the technology.

Keep the decision making at the local level and encourage more of it. Task the teams with deciding how they are going to enter and dominate a new market. Let them choose the technology they need to make it happen. The best thing you can do is ask them what they are doing with their time to get you competitive advantage instead of creeping elegance. You are not being a Luddite; you are being a good businessperson.

The Internet and other technologies offer you a great way to attract and entice your customers in the future. They can also suck up more resources than you can afford. For your growing business, think long and hard about how you use new technologies. Do you have the time and people to turn those technologies into an asset? Will they contribute to your box top or strip away some of your opportunities?

NOTES

1. Adapted from an article by Peter Meyer, "Controlling Costs," *Business & Economic Review,* October 1996.
2. Jeff Hawkins, interviewed by David Gewirtz in *PalmPower,* February 1, 1998. (www.palmpower.com)

CHAPTER ELEVEN

Applications: Plan for Technology and Take Advantage of the Disruption

Change can disrupt your business and your chances of getting to new opportunities quickly enough. Sane and sustainable growth will depend on how well you can harness disruption. The first step is to plan the disruption so it does the least harm. It makes even more sense to program the disruption so that it helps you and your customers. This will allow you to position your business to take the best advantage of new technologies.

TAKING ADVANTAGE OF DISRUPTION

Beyond investing in technology to conduct your business's operations, you can and should invest in technology to create and

Chart 11-1. Platform chart for sustainable warp-speed growth.

↑	Chapter 12	Warp-Speed Growth: Managing a Business Built for Speed							
	Chapters 7, 9, 11	APPLICA-TIONS ☞	Pricing	Tailoring	Prospective rewards	Indies	Prospective appraisals	Killer apps	Pain
	Chapters 6, 8, 10	INVEST-MENT STRATEGY ☞	Strategy—new markets		Strategy—recruiting and structure			Strategy—effect before technology (change is bad)	
	Chapters 1–5	WHAT TO INVEST ☞	Time		People			Money	
		WHERE TO INVEST ☞	Create, dominate new markets		Technology			People	
		FOUNDA-TION ☞	Jigsaw management—Building a box top Deciding and communicating what to work on and what to let go						

dominate new markets. So far, I have discussed the internal view; now, let's look at the market view with a focus on the Internet. Later in the chapter, I'll turn to enterprise technology.

Tremendous disruption will impact you and your customers' businesses as the variations of electronic commerce (e-commerce) roll out. Business patterns that have existed for years will change. Suppliers and customers on which you rely may disappear. Relationships will change, and some business transactions will speed up with or without you and your competitors. Markets that could not exist last year are possible now.

All of this change makes for opportunity. Your growth depends on whether you can take advantage of that opportunity. How you can you do so? Consider these two steps:

1. *Compare any new opportunity against your box top.* Because e-commerce will create more markets than you could ever enter, you will need to become very selective in investing your resources. This is a difficult discipline to enforce, but necessary. Again, look at your business and the networks as a large jigsaw puzzle. Before you start a puzzle of that size, you would always check the top of the box to see the picture that you are trying to match. You gain nothing by playing with pieces that do not fit into the puzzle. Playing with these pieces may be emotionally satisfying, but it wastes time, people, and money. When you are presented with a new market, use the jigsaw puzzle box top as your very restrictive guide. If you see an opportunity that looks great, measure it against the box top. No matter how appealing the new opportunity may seem, you need to resist the temptation to force it in or start your business over.

2. *Put your best people on the opportunities.* Rapidly growing businesses often hand this responsibility off to a data-proficient person from IS or staff who is not part of the business's mainstream. This is traditional but not correct. Ask your best people to become conversant with the fundamental network architectures and the choices. Use your best people to decide where to invest your time and theirs in the information superhighway. Ask your team to focus on your box top, not on the vendors' or technologists' box tops. New technologies and data networks will give you an opportunity to invest large amounts of time, people, and money—and to make big mistakes. You only have so many great people, and this is an important place to invest them. Make sure that you are not investing them in the wrong projects. Your business deserves the best people working only on the best opportunities.

BUILDING THE KILLER APPLICATION

What is a killer application (killer app)? It is a tool or feature so attractive and powerful that people will break habits to use it and pay a premium to get it. Killer apps are the holy grail of technology sales, just as they were the holy grail of many earlier products. Television did not sell itself, but *I Love Lucy* and Walter Cronkite may have sold millions of TV sets and supported billions of dollars of advertising. Lucille Ball and Walter Cronkite are examples of killer apps.[1]

However, just as most TV shows are not attractive enough to sell television sets, most attempts to develop a killer app fail. Let's look at efforts to develop Internet-related killer applications.

The Network Economy and Your Resources

The highest risk in creating new applications around the Internet is its lack of economic base. The Net does not pay for its own operations today, and despite all the forecasts and hopes, the Net is still a minor part of basic business. Today's stability relies on subsidies generated by the equities markets. This is not a stable or sustainable situation. Just as with physical structures, economic engines will always move to stability. Without enough income, the engine stops. It reaches entropy but in the virtual mode.

The Net is likely to achieve stability in one of three ways. The ugliest would be with a tremendous crash as the Net collapses in a flash of data storms around an inadequate infrastructure. With inadequate infrastructure support, the Net will fail increasingly often until users leave it for something more reliable. If this happens, your business will have wasted all the time and resources you have invested in Internet commerce.

A second form of stability would come from going to a regulated monopoly structure. The best example of this is the regulatory structure that allowed early phone service and cable television to survive and grow. This could seriously hamper businesses' ability to use the Net for creating new markets.

The third form of stability would come from accidentally stabilizing the Net with killer applications. This is the solution that most supporters are hoping for and working to deliver.

All this goes well beyond the issue of overvalued stocks. Even if the equity market stabilizes at a fraction of the overheated prices of the late 1990s, it will do little to support fundamental infrastructure investments. The fragility of the Internet's infrastructure is a consideration for any plan that would launch you into creating a new Net-based market. What will you do if the Internet fails?

Two other questions are: What will you do if someone develops a killer app? Will it make things better or worse for your growing business?

The Source of Killer Applications

Scott Kriens, president of Juniper Networks and a veteran of several market share wars, points to two models for using killer applications to open a new market: building into a coming change or building a solution that relieves a sudden pain.[2]

Building into a Coming Change

In the first model, you grow as the change does. The business of cable TV adapter boxes, for example, has grown as the cable TV market has increased. Coming changes are both slow and hard to predict, however. Many businesses build their fu-

Figure 11-1. Building a successful technology-based killer application.

The Two Models, With Their Pluses and Minuses
Model 1: Grow with Change + You can tag onto a trend. + You can predict timing (although not always well). − If the trend fails, so do you. − Change may not appear.   **Model 2: Create Pain** + You have some control over your destiny. + You define the playing field. − Some market control may be required. − It may be distasteful. − Anti-trust issues can arise.

Highest Risks
 	
  − You may create a solution in search of a problem.
  − The Internet may change in a way that no longer supports your business model.

ture on the expectation of a coming change and pay a high pen-
alty when it does not materialize. In the 1980s, 3Com designed
an entire corporate strategy around being the main independent
vendor of OS2 network software. When OS2 failed to become a
standard, the company was crippled and nearly destroyed.

The common denominator of failed killer apps is that they
were solutions to vendor concerns that the vendors hoped
would become solutions to consumer concerns. A number of
telephone companies and electronics suppliers have been looking for a way to cost-justify integrated services digital network
(ISDN) installations. ISDN is great for the phone companies. It
allows them to use existing wiring to deliver data to homes and
businesses, thereby saving the expense of replacing miles and
miles of wire beneath streets and on poles. The benefit to the
average user is not clear.

Movies on demand were to be the killer app that made the
information superhighway worth the investment for entertain-
ment companies. The Internet was to be the killer app that made
ISDN worth the expense for telephone companies. So far, both
have failed. They have not attracted enough users willing to pay
the premium required for the technology.

Forcing a Change Through Pain

A quick and sure way to create a killer application is to use
pain—to create enough pain that people *must* use it. This is a
time-tested way to get the best use of your resources. By creating
pain, you can predict how much time, people, and money you
will need to relieve the affliction. People who inflict pain in the
name of competition have been storied, respected, and reviled.
It has spawned lawsuits and success. Even if using pain is not
what you would choose, your business needs to consider it.
Someone else may do it to you and put your resources and
growth at risk.

Pain can create killer apps by accident. No one intentionally
decided to employ pain to build Symantec (owner of Norton
AntiVirus), Network Associates (formerly McAfee), and Dr. Sol-
omon's Software into half-billion-dollar companies. That happened when someone else started distributing computer viruses.

These companies responded to the pain with tools to detect and prevent viruses and repair the damage they cause. The *threat* of a virus is enough pain to sell a complex tool to people who do not really understand it. No one started viruses to create this market, and no one predicted that the market would develop. This is not always the case, however.

Consider the pain that made videotex workable in one country. Videotex is a concept that has been around for decades but has never achieved acceptance in major markets. Trials in the United States and other countries failed to create an economically viable product. Videotex has failed almost everywhere except in France.

What is different about France? In the United States, videotex was an incremental addition to existing services. Not so in Paris. Success did not come from the addition of a new service. Success came from the elimination of an old one. In France, videotex is supplied by the same people who supplied phone books. That supplier's new technology took off when that supplier stopped providing phone books. If you want a white-pages listing in France, the only choice that can provide accurate data is videotex. The supplier of videotex created the killer application by causing pain and then alleviating it.

But pain need not be created deliberately. Enough pain occurs naturally in business today to offer enormous opportunities to anyone who wants to build a killer app. The difference is between building a business plan to extend a product line and building a plan to address a large issue. If a problem "keeps people awake at night," a market exists.

Kriens points out that the latter makes better business sense. "If anything, I'd rather be the guy who suggests the benefit of solving a pain-induced problem than the one who proposes the gradual-change model. Observing pain, and the need for relief, is empirical and therefore a much stronger foundation to base a business model on."[3]

Your own style may or may not support the win-at-all-costs ethic. However, companies with the "Just win, baby," ethic could be the ones that save the Internet from economic chaos. How? By creating the pain that builds the case for the Net. That is what will generate killer applications when there is no natural market for them.

The Impact of Pain in Markets

There are many legal ways to create pain for customers and suppliers. You might create pain or even destroy a market with disruption. The disruption may be large, such as in 3Com's core markets. In the past decade, the number of network component providers has shrunk to only a few major players. The disruption can be small, such as when a Wal-Mart or Circuit City enters a new community. No market is too small or too large for a shakeout. Can you create one? George Day points out that "shake outs occur from an imbalance of capacity and demand."[4] Well, that can be arranged. A large player can suck up capacity or demand.

The logical places to look for that kind of strength are the loci of economic concentration. These loci are not always large. At the small end, look at Wal-Mart's entering a small community. At the larger end, the FDIC's market, banks, is shrinking fast. The result is a rapid increase in economic concentration.

Good management, mergers, intricate marketing alliances, and bankruptcies are building a class of powerhouses in many industries. Each of these industries has a few companies that are clearly dominant and able to change the rules of competition. These powerhouses are the ones that could accidentally make the Net viable or unusable for your business.

The effect of funding the Net infrastructure is unintentional. Except for Microsoft, none of the true economic powerhouses in the Western business world are interested in building a Net. They are interested in defining and dominating markets. Making the Net economically viable is a side effect.

For purposes of growing a business or division, consider medium-size industries that have experienced or are now experiencing rapid consolidation. Airlines, music distribution, and banking are the examples we'll examine in the following subsections. New markets may emerge from this consolidation, and many businesses that have grown rapidly will certainly fail as the disruption occurs. Another accidental by-product is the elimination of whole groups of businesses. As you look at these examples, consider where this kind of pain and response would leave your growing business. Saving the Internet might eliminate a business model on which you depend. You could be at risk.

Pain—Eliminating Airline Agent Ticketing

Airlines have enjoyed the dominant position in their distribution chain, but that is at risk. Consolidation in the industry has created a small set of powerful superagencies. Whereas individual agents and single-office agencies have little clout with an airline, large agencies can represent massive volumes of travelers. American Express (having bought Thomas Cook), Carlson (having merged with Wagonlit), and even cooperatives such as Woodside Travel Trust give these agencies a loud voice.

That loud voice has gotten a response from the carriers. Airlines have flexed their muscles effectively. They reduced the fees they pay to agencies several times in the 1990s. They have increased services to large buyers. For instance, if you deal directly with American Airlines, its reservation system may tell you how well your employees are observing your travel rules. It can provide you with detailed management information as it bypasses the local agency. Late in the 1990s, several airlines sold popular "back-to-back" tickets directly but penalized agents who did the same.[5]

Agencies are responding by getting closer to the customer, and if the agencies control the link to the customer, the airlines get nervous. Today, you and your business have an opportunity to bypass that link. You can buy travel by phone, by mail, or on the Internet. And you can get service across product and company lines. If you book a ticket with some carriers today, you can expect the carrier to ask whether you wish to rent a car. Today's technology allows an airline clerk (either electronic or real) to replace a travel agent.

Ed Perkins, former editor of *Consumer Reports Travel Letter*, notes, "It did not used to be, [but] with the electronic capabilities, an airline can now sell a ticket more cheaply than an agency [can]." The effect? "For the most part, this causes people to bypass travel agencies. Narrowly, to succeed, a small agency is going to have to get out of the business of issuing airline tickets completely."[6]

What would happen to travelers if United, Delta, and American all decided to stop paying any commissions to agencies for domestic travel? The agencies would face two options in selling you tickets: They could stop selling tickets for flights on the three largest carriers, or they could charge you an extra fee to obtain tickets for you. Pain is created. The options become a seat at the list price through the airline or the same seat through the agent, for 10 percent more. Either answer adds a new level of cost or inconvenience to you and your users. As Perkins notes, in this scenario, "small businesses are the people who wind up paying more for travel than anyone else. They are not big enough to sign a sweetheart deal with the airlines."

A nuisance beyond what the market would support? Not if the airlines put some thought and money into making it less painful to use a computer or phone than to use an agency or a travel department. Most airlines could present the entire travel package of air, car, and hotel in a single Web site. Today, most travelers and travel departments prefer paper tickets and agencies. They have no strong reason to change. Pain would provide that reason. If the big airlines stopped supporting agencies, users would have a strong reason to make that change. The Net could wind up with a killer application for business travelers—an application created by the infliction of pain elsewhere in the supply chain. That application could create an opportunity for your business growth—or stop it. Either way, the creation of pain by a dominant group of players would change how you allocate resources.

Pain—Eliminating Record Stores

A similar relationship exists between record companies and retailers. Record companies cannot survive by mail order or the Internet; they need retailer distribution. Retailers are adapting, and one adaptation has been to request and get cash payments for placement. When you see a poster in a store or a compact disc highlighted at a listening station, the manufacturer may have paid for that placement.

As the music market has flattened, it has caught record companies between stagnating revenues and increasing demands for cash payments to stores. Stores see increased competition and are looking to the record companies to help make up the shortfall. Neither side of the equation fully trusts the other.

Most of the major record companies have Web sites. Today you can download a snippet of music and perhaps order a recording. That may soon change. SONY has announced its plan to enable customers to purchase and download entire CDs. It has acquired a substantial presence on the Net, and other manufacturers are planning to do the same. Soon, if you want the latest Pink Floyd or Pavarotti, you can probably get it in less time than it would take to drive to the store.

What if three major record companies stopped paying placement fees and started raising wholesale prices without raising retail prices? What if they sold CDs online for two dollars less than discount retailers? Remember, these are the same companies that had the market strength nearly to eliminate vinyl records and replace them with compact discs.

Today, most consumers buy in record stores. They have no reason to change. However, if SONY, Atlantic, Warner, and others decided to undercut stores, consumers would have a strong reason to change their habits. It would be worth a great deal of infrastructure investment to the recording companies to change that habit and create a new market. The Internet would benefit but only as a side effect.

Pain—Eliminating Business and Personal Checking

The same kind of pain can occur in areas as prosaic as retail banking. Retail checking is very expensive for banks. One way to reduce costs would be to promote electronic banking. This is promising for the financial institutions. It has the potential to lower their costs and let them have the use of each customer's cash for an extra day or two. Banking by network would be a great boon to banks, but what's in it for users? Not much today, as electronic banking's lack of success has demonstrated.

But what if the large banks followed the lead of videotex in France and eliminated checks, offering electronic clearing as the only alternative? Today, small businesses have little reason to change to electronic banking. A decision by several major banks to cut costs by eliminating business checking would offer that reason. Network banking would become the tool of least pain.

As with any dislocation, these changes in distribution will allow some businesses to grow rapidly and will stunt the growth of others. Small travel agencies, retail record stores, and check printers may find that they are in positions where they cannot grow, victims of killer applications. Other companies will be building killer apps in a proactive manner, hoping to create and dominate new markets. Each owner or general manager has the option of trying to be in one position or the other.

Safety Valves—Contrary Forces to Deal With

If you decide to use pain as a way to grow your presence on the Net, consider the forces that work against this consolidation of power.

✧ *Ethics.* Creating pain to move customers from one platform to another clearly approaches what many would consider to be unethical behavior. To wipe out travel agencies or consumer checking to gain a few points of margin may be dishonorable, but that won't stop people from trying it. A discussion of right versus wrong is unlikely to make a big difference.

✧ *Hubris.* As powerful as major companies are, few are as powerful as they think. That gives them the opportunity to overstretch and fail. It happened to 3Com when it tried to dictate the format for modems running at 56,000 bits per second. American Airlines failed when it tried to change the pricing structure of the airline industry in the mid-1990s. If you decide to inflict pain in a distribution structure, make sure your actual strength matches your self-image.

✧ *Entropy.* Cabals and artificial market structures are subject to the same effects as mountains and buildings: They fall down (fail) due to entropy. Many business structures have failed over a period of decades as they stagnated. The same could happen to any pain-centered program to move people to the Internet. If no one renews the business structure on an ongoing basis, it will become ineffective in short order.

✧ *Legislation.* If Congress and the states are willing to consider regulating fees on ATMs, they might also choose to regulate other uses of e-commerce, such as the airline ticketing, music retailing, and bank account scenarios discussed earlier in this section. However, you might not wish to rely on this—legislatures are notoriously hard to predict or control.

In short, if your business is thinking of creating a pain-based killer application, it will face the institutional forces summarized in Figure 11-2. Of these forces, the main threats to a pain-oriented killer app come from the sponsoring companies themselves.

APPLYING THESE INSIGHTS TO BUSINESS GROWTH

Many companies will work hard to use technology to design a killer app in order to create and then dominate markets. If you are using this strategy, pay careful attention to the risks identified in Figure 11-1. This includes the risk of fragility in the Net.

A good place to start is to choose carefully between the two strategies in Figure 11-1. If you choose the pain strategy, make sure that you are working on something that will highlight a real problem, not an issue that will not be meaningful. On the other hand, you should choose a problem that customers per-

Figure 11-2. Relative forces that work against technology-based killer applications.

If your business is creating a killer app based on pain, here are some institutional forces that work against it:	
Force	Potency
Ethical considerations	Weak
Hubris	Strong
Entropy	Moderate (but by the time it weakens, your business could be gone)
Legislation	Weak

ceive with or without your assistance. The point is not to be Machiavellian; it is to bring to market a solution that performs a real service.

Even if your business is unable to create a market by developing a killer application, you should take some steps to promote your own growth. If you do not, you run the risk of being eliminated by someone else's attempt to create a new market or a killer app. Consider two possibilities:

1. You are strong enough in your market to be able to create pain for a distribution layer or channel.
2. You can't control your distribution chain.

For example, in the first case, the airlines are well positioned to use dominance to create pain for agencies. If you can create this level of pain, you can look to the Net to eliminate a layer of cost from your business. Or the Net can become a tool for you to use to get closer to your customers.

If your business is in a position of market power, you can either sponsor others or make it painful for them to be in business. Which you choose depends on your box top. For example, 3Com has chosen to sponsor a strong development community for the Palm products, which benefits the users. Although the company rarely sells hardware directly to users, it does try to supply software and applications directly. It works to create a strong connection with its users.

In the second case, ask what you can do for your customers that the other channels cannot. Television stations are an example of the situation in which your business is not dominant. If you run a TV station, you are not able to dominate either your suppliers (the networks, syndicators, or local producers) or your customers. You cannot change the economic model or even create much pain for others. You are part of a distribution chain that develops little original content.

If you are part of a distribution chain, build a plan on the assumption that someone could eliminate you from the chain. When you can, move your business from the distribution chain to a place where you can control the pain. If you distribute for others, find a market niche where you can be the creator or manufacturer. Occupy a spot where the end users cannot do without you. Try to change to the creator/manufacturer position and become indispensable to the customers. Although this means that your business must change its box top, this is a much better platform from which to grow.

Using Technology to Build Markets

To look at a logical way to create a new technology market, let's return to the discussion of buying technology for your own operational uses. If you consider how you would best run your own growing business, you can apply that to how your customers might accept or decline your new market entry. For an example of such a technology, let's examine network computing (NC).[7] As a customer, you get new offers from suppliers constantly. Every week, someone offers you the latest technology. The question is how to deal quickly but correctly with the choice.[8]

The normal assumption made by vendors is that you would look at NC as a tool to drive down costs. As a customer, you might instead ask, What is NC to a growing business?

Look at a network computer as two different products. First, a network computer is a computer costing less than $400 that allows your people to work as though they had a $4,000 computer.[9] The network computer has no floppy or CD drive and little memory. It relies on your network or on the Internet for its programs and information.

Second, the network computer concept is a highly promoted effort to either reduce the market presence of Microsoft and Intel or reinforce it.

What would an NC solution look like if you installed it? Your users would have something a little smarter than a terminal on each desk. The new computers would get their intelligence from servers on a network or the Internet. They would have to rely on an intranet or on the Internet because they can do very little by themselves.

Do You Care If It Saves Money?

For most buyers, the first question is, "Will it save money?" The answer is, "Not as much as advertised." The cost to acquire a network computer is low. You might save as much as $3,600 per machine. Because the software is on the network instead of the PC, you save because you are freed from the need to upgrade each machine every time new products appear. You only upgrade your copies on the network servers. And because the network computer has almost nothing in it, the cost of maintenance will slowly drop as the operating system becomes stable.

However, most software designed for network use requires more training, not less. Not only will you have to pay out-of-pocket expenses, but when you ask an employee to switch to a network computer, you will lose his or her productivity during days of retraining and relearning. That opportunity cost could easily exceed all the other savings from network computing. When your people are learning software commands, they are not taking care of your business. Taking your people away from the box top is your greatest cost.

The next largest cost may be your networking. Each network computer will be online all the time it's in use. That means a larger investment in modems, cable, phone lines, Ethernet (or its equivalent), and network management.

The cost of software is not likely to go down even though you just buy copies for the servers. Your business can choose from only a few good office packages for network use, and their price is higher than you would like.

More important than money: Will your people stand for it? They are used to being productive in a certain way with certain tools. Do you and other employees use laptops when you're on the road? Do your people work from home in the evenings and on weekends? Will NC hinder that productivity?

You can expect this to be a problem until Microsoft, Word-Perfect, and IBM produce NC products identical to PC software. Some of your people have tailored their macros, toolbars, spell checkers, and other features. Don't make your users switch between two different tool sets. Time is the most expensive resource you have; don't spend it on making your people relearn what they are already doing well. If people are the second most critical resource, don't invest them in a process that does not make them more effective. It's easy to make machines more efficient at the cost of making people less effective. Avoid this mistake.

The Decision Process

When making decisions about investing time, people, and money in technologies, the place to start is with the effects those investments deliver for your business. Cost savings do not provide the value to your business. The value comes from the effect you get from your investment. If all you wanted was to save money, you would still be using computers with Intel 286 processors and running WordPerfect 5.1 for DOS. Because saving money is not your principal reason to be in business, start with what your reasons are.

The reasons to be in business are part of your organization's box top. That will direct you toward the effects of technology, not the costs or building blocks. When you decide to leave old technology, the objective is to get an effect your business needs. That effect comes more from software than from hardware. So should your decision to invest scarce resources in technologies. Your business may be forced to consider a change, but that does not mean that the process for choosing technologies would change.

Figure 11-3. Savings and costs for network computers.

Savings
+ Up to $3,600 per workstation (including software licensing)
+ Reduction in ongoing maintenance costs for PC hardware
+ Reduced cost to upgrade software

Costs
− Opportunity cost from training
− Cost of disruption from new tools and implementation issues
− Higher network hardware and software costs
− More people to maintain and manage the network
− More expensive software
− Reduced productivity from laptops and home

Using network computers as an example, the four steps would be as follows:

1. Let your box top guide you to the appropriate software. What programs will deliver the effect you need in order to grow your business?

2. Look at the available and proven software that meets your needs and can run on a network with network computers *without* disrupting your users.

3. Then look at the support for that software. Is the supplier really committed to network computing, or is it waiting to see whether anyone buys this stuff? Can you get good, knowledgeable support?

4. If you are comfortable about the preceding issues, consider cost issues, as shown in Figure 11-3 on page 195.

Then you will know whether investing in network computers makes sense.

The same process can be followed in making decisions about other technology that you are considering. No matter how attractive the technology you may be offered in the coming years, the key decisions remain the same.

Implications for New Markets

If your business wishes to create and dominate a new market with technology, you have an opportunity to set margin con-

Figure 11-4. Four steps wise customers follow when evaluating new technology.

1. Do the products provide the effect that is needed from the user's perspective?
2. Is disruption minimal, as the user sees it?
3. Does the proposition feel right? Does it make sense? Is the vendor credible?

And then

4. Is the purchase cost-effective?

straints aside and achieve rapid and sustainable growth. The key to the use of technology is to remember that this is only a tool, for both you and your customer.

If your customer follows the four steps to decide what to implement (Figure 11-4), you would be wise to do the same. Effect will always be the first criterion, and cost is the last. American Airlines did not create frequent-flyer programs, investing thousands of person-years and millions of dollars, to save money. It instituted these programs to get an effect.

If you want to create and dominate a new market with technology, start with the effect to be delivered by that technology. If delivering that effect means producing a less elegant product, do that. The box top for sustainable growth will include creating a desirable technology for the sake of delivering a specified effect, not for the sake of using the technology.

NOTES

1. Much of this section first appeared in the article by Peter Meyer, "Killer Applications," *Business & Economic Review*, January 1998.
2. Conversation with the author, summer 1997.
3. Ibid.
4. "Strategies for Surviving a Shakeout," *Harvard Business Review*, March 1997, p. 92.
5. Susan Carey "Airlines Crack Down on Agents Over Fare Ploys," *Wall Street Journal*, September 12, 1997.
6. Conversation with the author, November 7, 1997.
7. At the time this book was written, network computing was available, but Web-hosted applications were not yet widely available. This discussion would apply to application service providers (ASPs) if Web-hosted applications were offered.
8. This section appeared in a similar form in the article by Peter Meyer, "A Network Computer for Your Business?" *Business & Economic Review*, April 1998.
9. Throughout this discussion, the dollar figures are estimates.

CHAPTER TWELVE

Warp-Speed Growth: Managing a Business Built for Speed

Rapid, sustainable, and sane growth is certainly possible. Warp speed will never be easy, but it can be very satisfying for general managers and owners. It can happen for both independent businesses and divisions of corporations. However, as you grow, you may wonder how far you can go.

ARE THERE LIMITS TO RAPID GROWTH?

Despite what we might want, warp-speed growth isn't always infinite. Rapid growth is not constrained by the boundaries that you might expect, however. Although most limits to growth are expressed in terms of markets and money, these are not the real constraints to sustained rapid growth. The limitation to be concerned with is how the management team performs its role. Let's look at that now.

Do Finite Markets Limit Growth?

Markets will always saturate because, for every product, the number of consumers is limited. Even sales of over-the-counter pain medication will reach a natural ceiling. The world has a finite number of people who have aches and can afford to treat them.

Of course, a business can still grow in a finite market. One way to continue growth is to increase penetration in the market. If you produce pharmaceuticals, you may choose to build demand-creation programs to help prospective consumers recognize the aches that your medication can mask. You may choose to extend a brand (line extension), offering slightly different options, such as coated pills, gel caps, or different combinations of pain and allergy relief. You can allow unit sales to remain flat but increase your prices. Demand creation, line extensions, and price hikes are good, but they only increase sales in a defined market. Eventually, your business will reach market saturation, and growth in that market will stop.

However, market saturation need not be the check on your business. International Business Machines (IBM) continued to grow even as the large computer market seemed to slow. Ford continued to grow even as the U.S. market for cars seemed to saturate. Microsoft continues to grow despite flattening sales in personal computers. These three companies have done this by moving beyond their original markets to create (and then hope to dominate) new markets.

The decision to sustain rapid growth is often a commitment to avoid market limitations by creating and dominating new markets. The limit on your growth changes. It goes from your ability to penetrate existing markets to your ability to create and dominate new markets.

As originally illustrated in Chapter 6 (Figure 6-2), to move into new markets, your business can follow either of two good paths:

Two Paths to New Markets

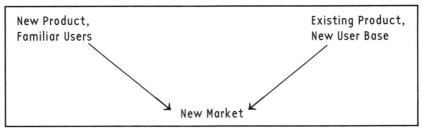

1. Build a new product and sell it to the users you know and understand.
2. Take the existing products and look for new users.

Each path is difficult, but both work. Ford chose to take existing products to new user bases by exporting its basic cars to other countries. Ford's growth in the late 1990s often came from international sales. IBM has used both paths over time. Although these companies have not always been consistent, they have both managed to return to rapid growth.

Does Finite Money Limit Growth?

When I ask managers what limits their growth, access to money is a common answer. Lack of funds is a comfortable response but not a good one. You can find many ways to get more money, just as this book has shown many techniques to get more people and time. The problem is that when you find more money, you may not have overcome the limits to growth.

Consider StrataCom, the company we examined in Chapter 5. When StrataCom was growing rapidly in the 1990s, it became clear to the executives that the limit to growth was not money. The company had plenty of that coming in. The limitation was people and time. As several executives told me, the company could not hire fast enough to fill all the needs for growth. If StrataCom could not get more results from the same people, the company was destined to stop growing.

Consider TWA, an airline that has gotten considerable funding over the years. Despite injections of cash, the company has not succeeded at rapid growth. The reasons are arguable, but lack of money has not been one of them.

Automation is one way to increase productivity—use cash to supplement people. Managing people well is a better way—get your teams to do only the most important work.

What Is the Role of the Owner or General Manager in Avoiding Growth Limits?

What is your role as present or future owner or manager? The owner or general manager has the responsibility to make sure the management team:

✧ Clearly defines success before the project starts (sets the box top as defined in Chapter 2)

✧ Doesn't invest time, people, or money in projects and products that fall outside that box top

Thomas Watson Sr. (the founder and first CEO of IBM) is almost as famous for one inaccurate market prediction as for his ability not to let that forecast limit the company. When he forecast a worldwide market of only five large computers, he did not tell his team that they could not go after other markets.

IBM's ability to bounce up against and move around definition limits has been a function of management. When the market for renting large computers dried up through government intervention, the company was able to redefine the product to work with the users it knew best. The company converted monthly access to ownership, still selling to the same information technology (IT) customers.

Remember, the product was not computers; it was access to fast applied computations and the software to run them. The company rented access at first and then moved to selling hardware when the consent decree restricted rentals.

Your product is everything you present to a customer, from the sales literature through the ordering/invoicing process to the support team. Consider aircraft engines. As John Newhouse points out in *The Sporty Game,* the decision to buy billions of dollars worth of airplanes has often come down to the willingness of an engine company to offer attractive financial terms to an airline.[1] Knowing which terms to offer and how to present them is a function of management, not technology.

The redefinition of the IBM product was not a technology or development issue; it was a management issue. The computers did not change, nor did the software. IBM's product was a combination of hardware, software, and packaging. This product, like most, includes financial terms and support—which were defined by management, not by the software and hardware technologists.

The decision to try and create a new market is not a technology or financial choice; it is a management judgment. In IBM's case, as the large computer systems market looked as though it might saturate, the company helped create and dominate other markets. From this side of the millennium, it may be hard to remember that IBM was the company that made personal computers acceptable. Apple, Osborne, and others were faster to market, but IBM was first to acceptance.

IBM's growth was a function not of markets but of the management team's ability to move the business outside the definitions of existing markets. At each junction, the team had to move resources to the right projects and efforts, and to keep that work focused. As the company mounted a resurgence in the 1990s, it did the same thing, shedding resource investments that fell outside the box top and adding more time and people to other efforts. The teams at IBM did not invent electronic commerce over the Internet, but by the turn of the century, many people thought that it had. IBM did not achieve that market acceptance with money. The company made it happen by investing the right people in a short time frame and telling them to ignore the other parts of the company.

In the same way, Palm Computing created a new market for handheld digital assistants. The company was not first to market with a complete device, but Palm was the first to gain market acceptance. (See Chapter 10 for a discussion of Palm's box top.) Through the late 1990s and into this century, it has dominated the market despite concerted efforts by much larger companies. This dominance comes from management decisions to:

* Build a box top.
* Focus the available resources on the pieces that fit in that box top and not on the pieces that fall outside that picture.

While competitors focused on filling expansion slots and duplicating complex computer software, Palm Computing put its time, people, and money into simplicity and a nearly intuitive user interface. The growth of the Palm product sales is not just measured in the number of people who want organizers. Those consumers will be supplemented by users from different markets. Whether these new users are corporations that want to distribute handheld systems or users who want to have wireless access to data such as plane and movie schedules, the company is stretching the markets for its products each year.

For Palm Computing, IBM, Ford, and other companies that are growing rapidly, the challenge will not be money or markets. The challenge will be to allocate people, time, and then money to the right work. Any of the good people in your organization can do good work with limited resources, but only the senior executives can tell them where to invest the time, the people, and the money. That is the present or future role of the reader of this book.

Chart 12-1. Platform chart for sustainable warp-speed growth.

Chapter 12	*Warp-Speed Growth: Managing a Business Built for Speed*							
Chapters 7, 9, 11	APPLICATIONS ☞	Pricing	Tailoring	Prospective rewards	Indies	Prospective appraisals	Killer apps	Pain
Chapters 6, 8, 10	INVESTMENT STRATEGY ☞	Strategy— new markets		Strategy—recruiting and structure			Strategy— effect before technology (change is bad)	
Chapters 1–5	WHAT TO INVEST ☞	Time		People			Money	
	WHERE TO INVEST ☞	Create, dominate new markets		Technology			People	
	FOUNDATION ☞	*Jigsaw management—Building a box top Deciding and communicating what to work on and what to let go*						

WHERE DO YOU START?

In your business, time, people, and money will always be limited. Those limitations will always stand between you and the results you want. To get those specific results, start with a box top. That view of where you are going can define where you want to invest the business's resources.

Where do you start? Once you have your box top, ask yourself and your team some questions. You might start with:

- ✧ Could you be creating and dominating a new market?
- ✧ Are you building products that involve your customers—products that they can tailor to themselves?
- ✧ Could you grow more sanely if you went after Indies instead of employees?
- ✧ Is the technology becoming more important than what it does?
- ✧ Are you conserving time, people, and money to invest in new opportunities?
- ✧ Does your box top tell you which opportunities are the right ones in which to invest those resources?

Figure 12-1. Resources, strategies, and applications.

For sustainable growth, apply your resources to strategies, using the strategies to define which applications you invest in.		
Resources:	Strategies:	
Time	New markets	
People →	Technology →	Applications
Money	People	

To achieve sustainable and sane warp-speed growth, take these five steps:

1. *Build a box top.* Invest time to define success criteria and limit options. Doing this will enable you to avoid the crazy-making insanity of wasting time, people, and money on work that really does not matter.

2. *Consider creating and dominating a market.* You might choose to propose a new product to known users or a known product to customers you do not yet know. Either way, the opportunity for growth is great, as are the risks. A lower-risk path might be to enter an existing market with a technology or people advantage. Choosing the path focuses your view of the box top.

3. *Balance your resources and build an investment plan.* Time, people, and money will be the assets that can fund the effort in new markets, technology, or people. Look carefully at each resource and build the strategy that delivers the best result at the lowest cost in time, people, and money.

4. *Act to conserve your resources for better investments.* As the team rolls out the applications of the strategy, always ask whether you can find a better way to invest and use your limited resources. Conserve them for new opportunities.

5. *Have fun.* The rewards of sustainable, sane growth should be personal as well as corporate.

Warp-speed growth will always be difficult, and at times you may wonder why you are bothering with such monumental effort. When that doubt occurs, look at the box top, your specific goals. If they are important, you'll have that flash of fun and pleasure that provides motivation for you and your team. Expect to lose motivation over time, and be ready with that box top, the view of what success and its benefits will look like. You will all appreciate it.

Ask yourself what you enjoy. Sanity does not come from doing every last thing that can be done. Work on the top two or three issues in your box top. Teams that limit the scope of what they wish to do and then do the selected things well achieve warp speed consistently. They invest time, people, and money in the best strategies. You can do just as well.

Note

1. John Newhouse, *The Sporty Game* (New York: Knopf, 1982).

Index

About the Author

Peter Meyer is a principal in The Meyer Group, a management consulting firm that specializes in helping companies grow rapidly, and in a way that they can sustain. Located in Scotts Valley, CA, the firm works on growth opportunities with clients in the Fortune 500, overseas, and in start-up mode. The common denominator to each is that the owner or manager wants to plan for and achieve manageable growth.

Peter is also a popular speaker and the author of a number of articles on growing businesses. His work has appeared in the *Wall Street Journal, Business Horizons,* the *Canadian Business Review, Business Communications Review, Dateline, Executive Female, Solutions,* and *Leader to Leader.* He is a contributing editor for the *Business & Economic Review.*

Besides national television and radio appearances, he has spoken to executive and management groups in the United States, Europe, South America, Asia, and Australia. He is also a frequent guest on hosted Internet chats on a variety of sites and online services.

For more information, and the latest articles by Peter, check the company web site at http://www.MeyerGrp.com. For more copies of this book, please check your local bookseller, one of the online services, the Meyer Group, or visit the American Management Association and AMACOM online at http://www.amanet.org.

DATE DUE

			Printed in USA

HIGHSMITH #45230